### THE CASE FOR COMMONWEALTH FREE TRADE

By

Brent Cameron

© Copyright 2005 Brent Cameron
All rights reserved. No part of this publication may be reproduced, stored in a retrieval system, or transmitted, in any form or by any means, electronic, mechanical, photocopying, recording, or otherwise, without the written prior permission of the author.

Note for Librarians: a cataloguing record for this book that includes Dewey Decimal Classification and US Library of Congress numbers is available from the Library and Archives of Canada. The complete cataloguing record can be obtained from their online database at:
www.collectionscanada.ca/amicus/index-e.html
ISBN 1-4120-4277-1
Printed in Victoria, BC, Canada

# TRAFFORD

*Offices in Canada, USA, Ireland, UK and Spain*
This book was published *on-demand* in cooperation with Trafford Publishing. On-demand publishing is a unique process and service of making a book available for retail sale to the public taking advantage of on-demand manufacturing and Internet marketing. On-demand publishing includes promotions, retail sales, manufacturing, order fulfilment, accounting and collecting royalties on behalf of the author.

**Book sales for North America and international:**
Trafford Publishing, 6E–2333 Government St.,
Victoria, BC v8T 4P4 CANADA
phone 250 383 6864 (toll-free 1 888 232 4444)
fax 250 383 6804; email to orders@trafford.com

**Book sales in Europe:**
Trafford Publishing (UK) Ltd., Enterprise House, Wistaston Road Business Centre, Wistaston Road, Crewe, Cheshire CW2 7RP UNITED KINGDOM
phone 01270 251 396 (local rate 0845 230 9601)
facsimile 01270 254 983; orders.uk@trafford.com

**Order online at:**
www.trafford.com/robots/04-2084.html

10 9 8 7 6 5 4 3 2 1

For Jodi, Ethan and Sloane

*Table of Contents*

Chapter 1: The Case for
          Commonwealth Free Trade     1

Chapter 2: Why Commonwealth
          Free Trade?                 13

Chapter 3: The History of
          Empire & Commonwealth
          Trade                       31

Chapter 4: Objective of the
          CFTA
                                      66
Chapter 5: Economic
          Opportunities
          for a CFTA                  73

Chapter 6: The Lomé Example           85

Chapter 7: Commonwealth Trade
          Cooperation                 94

Chapter 8: CFTA Organization          130

Chapter 9: Preconditions for
          Membership                  136

Chapter 10: CFTA
          Implementation              142

Chapter 11: CFTA and
          Development Aid             146

Chapter 12: CFTA and the
          United States               157

Chapter 13: CFTA and the WTO          175

Chapter 14: CFTA and the EU           184

| | |
|---|---|
| Chapter 15: 'Network Trading' | 192 |
| Chapter 16: The Way Forward? | 195 |
| Chapter 17: Conclusion | 202 |
| List of Appendices | 209 |
| Bibliography | 223 |
| Index | 229 |

# ACKNOWLEDGMENTS

The author wishes to thank a number of people who, either directly or indirectly, gave me the encouragement and inspiration to pursue this work, and the confidence to push forward at the risk of what critics might say. When one gets past the initial eagerness of pursuing a project like this, thoughts turn to whether it has any particular value beyond the personal desire for expression.

I would like to offer a special thanks to Markus Reichardt for being both a cheerleader and outspoken critic in just the right measure.

Also, I would like to offer my appreciation to John Coburn Evans, Jim Alcock, Nick Thompson, and Ben Matthews, among others, who have offered encouragement and assistance in this project. The efforts of Laura Pringle and Bill Mitchell at Trafford Publishing are also worthy of note.

In particular, I am thankful for the love and support of my wife and children. It is because of them that my endeavours are invested with meaning. They have made me feel that no matter what I may wish to pursue, those dreams have validity and purpose in of themselves. Without them, and their confidence in me, I might never have felt myself capable of such an undertaking.

The idea for this work came from nothing more elaborate than noticing countries, and peoples, sharing so many traits, and all concerned about similar issues. It seems a truism of any successful relationship, whether at the individual level, or in the field of politics, that if two or more have the same likes, dislikes, hopes and fears, and can benefit by working together, then those connections are worth pursuing. Certainly, in the realm of the theoretical, where all things are possible, we can open our minds to such opportunities.

As with any honest writer, the more valid and illuminating aspects of this book are due, in no small part, to the guidance of others. Errors and shortcomings are the domain of the author.

BHC
Yarker, Ontario, Canada
February, 2005

# GLOSSARY

**ACCP** – Assembly of Caribbean Community Parliamentarians

**ACP** – Africa, Caribbean and Pacific (states)

**AGOA** – African Growth and Opportunities Act (USA)

**ANZCERTA** – Australia-New Zealand Closer Economic Relations Treaty

**BWI** – British West Indies

**CAP** – Common Agricultural Policy (European Union)

**CARICOM** – Caribbean Economic Community

**CARIFTA** – Caribbean Free Trade Association

**CBC** – Commonwealth Business Council

**CDB** – Caribbean Development Bank

**CFTA** – Commonwealth Free Trade Association

**CFTC** - Commonwealth Fund for Technical Cooperation

**COL** – Commonwealth of Learning

**CSC** – Commonwealth Science Council

**ECOWAS** – Economic Community of West African States

**EEC** – European Economic Community

**EU** – European Union

**FDI** – Foreign Direct Investment

**GATT** – General Agreement on Tariffs and Trade

**GDP** – Gross Domestic Product

**G8** – Group of Eight Industrialized Nations

**IMF** – International Monetary Fund

**NAFTA** – North American Free Trade Agreement

**NEPAD** – New Economic Partnership for Africa's Development

**OECD** – Organization for Economic Cooperation and Development

**OECS** - Organization of Eastern Caribbean States

**SACU** – Southern Africa Customs Union

**TIAF** – Trade and Investment Access Facility
**US** – United States
**USSR** – Union of Soviet Socialist Republics
**WTO** – World Trade Organization

*Chapter 1*

THE CASE FOR COMMONWEALTH FREE TRADE

The post-Cold War world, already more than a decade old, is still in its nascent stage of development. Despite the boldly optimistic claims of a 'new world order', or in the words of Francis Fukuyama "the end of history," the victory of Western capitalism over communism has not ushered in a utopian era of peace, prosperity and stability for the majority of the world's peoples.

The portent of this bold prediction was similar to that of the Marxist vision it replaced, insofar as it imagined a world finally at peace with itself under one economic system. While capitalism is arguably more amenable to this desired outcome, it must function in tandem with political ideologies that are equally up to the challenge. This is what makes the difference between being a citizen and a unit of consumption.

# 2

Without the political infrastructure to support economic freedom, many countries have been deprived of the opportunity to compete in the global marketplace, while most are continually forced to make choices between what may be best for their citizens, and what may be best for their alliances.

Pragmatists will rightly counter that societies do not live by ideology or dogma alone. National, or societal, interests do matter. Disproving a people's chosen form of government does not invalidate the people themselves. Russia without communism is still Russia – just administered to different rules. What has not changed is the collective desire of a people that those rules make one's general status and state of affairs improve.

The end of the Cold War has essentially meant bringing international relations full circle to a point predating the path that determined the 20$^{th}$ century. Our world, despite its technological advancements and the lessons of history, more resembles that which had been cobbled together in the aftermath of the Napoleonic Wars – the "Concert of Europe."

National interests, not political ideology, have always informed foreign policy, but not in such an unvarnished way, which has not happened in our lifetimes. As a result, it is a period of time that calls upon the talents of historians as much as it does economists or political scientists.

What truly distinguishes this period from its predecessor is that economic and military stability is not guaranteed by a balance of power. It is guaranteed by one power possessing an unchallenged hegemony on both measures. It is guaranteed by the United States.

One can rightly argue that given the examples of history, as well as the possible alternatives, that America is a better steward of this power and responsibility than any other nation or empire under comparable conditions. But while it is true that if the world is to be unipolar, better it be the United States than another, it still begs the question whether a unipolar world is preferable to a more balanced regime. A colony of the most enlightened, most benevolent empire is still but a colony – limited in means and in opportunity to express its will at home, and its values abroad.

Nations, by their very nature, respond to the pressures of their domestic constituency. Former Speaker of the US House of Representatives Tip O'Neill put it more succinctly when he said that "all politics is local." An international system based on American power is an international system that responds primarily to the needs and interests of the American electorate. Decisions impacting the lives and livelihoods of people from Ottawa to Brisbane, London to Chennai, become secondary considerations as American voters weigh their decision as to who will lead the world's only superpower. In many respects, this state of affairs constitutes the underlying problem for those opposed to globalization, viewing it as nothing more than an entrenchment of American economic and political power.

The 'high' issues of war and peace, while grabbing the headlines, constitute a small element of this emerging international agenda. Trade and development are the real substance of concern among the nations of the world; that is, how one expects to earn their daily bread. Indeed, the majority of concordant bodies within the framework of the United Nations, from the International Labour Organization (ILO) to the World Trade Organization (WTO), are concerned with issues of trade and development.

It is in this milieu that the real competition between nations, and regional blocs, is beginning to translate itself. The pursuit of territory is no longer integral to securing resources. Indeed, given the human and material costs of armed conflict, it is as inefficient as it is immoral. It is not ownership *per se*, but access to, and control of, resources, capital, technology and markets that determines winners and losers in the new globalized marketplace.

Nations that lack the ability to compete with larger powers in this brave new world have traditionally acceded to them, or banded together in common cause with other smaller powers – the hope that the subsequent pooling of resources would create a mass large enough to resist such pressures. This latter option creates a relationship that gives its members the geopolitical equivalent of "economies of scale." Both choices involve their own unique sets of compromises and accommodations. Trade access and economic development require a reciprocity that often hits at the heart of a nation's ability to set rules and standards.

For sovereign states, however, access to markets and capital is simply not enough. In order to preserve the basic tenets of democracy and the legal legitimacy of nation-states, any multilateral relationship must be equal and mutual. Parties must be willing to agree that, beyond a set of rules to facilitate and regulate their commerce, each exercises the right to use its political mandate subject only to the pressures of its own citizens and the accepted tenets of civil society.

Current international trading regimes have a mixed record on this count. Some, like the WTO, in order to achieve the broadest possible consensus, reduce agreements to a compromise of the lowest common denominator. The reality of reaching consensus among over 100 nations of varying degrees of economic and military might, cultures and systems of government means that final agreements are inevitably minimalist in their scope and impact. Moreover, when they do seek to make a stand, it often offends the sensibilities and political traditions of specific states – such as the policy of considering "culture" as a commercial commodity. Also, in these situations, there appears to be a correlation between the level of influence and resources of a given state, and their degree of satisfaction at the outcome of such negotiations.

Other agreements, on the other hand, take on a far more ambitious agenda – that of integration and the eventual creation of a supra-state authority, such as the EU. While very successful in harmonizing trade, they achieve this end by attempting to harmonize politics between member states, thereby eroding the power of national governments to set policies and implement programs, even if those initiatives are supported by a broad domestic coalition. Furthermore, these authorities are generally regional in nature, and as successful as they may be in reducing barriers to trade and investment within their area, they do little to continue this trend outside their zone. It may actually be argued that they merely give rise to an escalation of predatory and aggressive trade actions. Protectionism between nations-states disappears, only to be replaced by protectionism between regional trading blocs.

Still others, such as the agreements between the European Union and the African, Caribbean, and Pacific states, known as the ACP grouping – the so-called Lomé Conventions – create an 'economic mentorship' between industrialized and developing nations. This series of agreements, however, is based on an architecture that merely perpetuates the paternalism that the developed world has fought against since many of those states underwent the transformation from colony to sovereign nation.

And so nation states wishing to increase trade and prosperity for their peoples are currently served by three alternatives: to commit to a global, multilateral process which is still dominated by more powerful states and achieves consensus through small, cumbersome steps; to sign bilateral agreements with more affluent and powerful nations, inevitably seceding some degree of sovereignty and national determination to secure access to markets; or to sacrifice national sovereignty altogether to join a regional quasi-governmental bloc – assuming that one would be able to join in the first place.

Such choices are inadequate for sovereign peoples and democratic states, and that the quest for access to markets and capital should not demand such trade-offs.

If we accept the following premises: that freer trade is a desired outcome; that freer trade outside, and between, trading blocs provides greater opportunities for businesses and individuals; and that nation-states still have a valid democratic role, then we must look to reinventing the network of existing trading relationships. As Britain's Chancellor of the Exchequer, Gordon Brown, has stated "The key challenge now is to devise procedures and institutions - nothing less than new international rules of the game - that help deliver greater stability, and prosperity for all our citizens in industrialized and industrializing economies alike."[1]

For the vast majority of the world's nations, a new trading relationship must be a clear improvement on the status quo. Numerous attempts in the past to bring the developing world fully into the global economy have failed for a myriad of reasons, with each failure engendering cynicism and a loss of faith in finding a lasting solution. What is needed is a new trading structure that builds on existing relationships between nations, is able to fulfill many

---

[1] Brown, Rt. Hon. Gordon, "*New Global Structures for the New Global Age*," The Round Table (1999), #349, p.40

policy objectives, including trade, and yet preserve the integrity of domestic political and social institutions.

In order to improve trade and commerce prospects at home and abroad, without sacrificing the sovereign and democratic rights of a people, one must devise a trading regime that demands only those compromises and concessions that allow an association to be productive and effective. Based on a Charter of Common Values and Practices, it must be a forum of independent nations committed to a mutually respectful relationship – one that transcends the boundaries of regionalism or degree of development.

The success of such an enterprise, however, depends on a degree of compatibility among its partners. While not necessarily equating the national interest identically, member states should expect a certain degree of commonality on as many levels as possible. The more traits that nations share, the easier it is to attempt some amount of economic cooperation and coordination.

Already there exists an international organization of nation-states that share much common ground – language, cultural reference points, and systems of government and jurisprudence. It comprises over 50 nations and more than 1/3 of the world's population. Despite frequent challenges, it has, for more than a half-century, served as an important forum for the discussion of human rights, development, culture and sport.

The Commonwealth of Nations presents an existing multi-lateral framework from which one may devise a trading association that embraces rich and poor nations from around the globe, increasing trade and development while preserving the political integrity of its member-states. Not only does this organization provide the 'critical mass' necessary for a trade association to be viable, it is of sufficient scope and diversity as to allow it a significant voice in the broader debates over trade liberalization and the very nature of globalization.

It is, therefore, the thesis of this work to discuss the merits of creating a Commonwealth Free Trade Association (CFTA), a trading relationship comprised of nation-states belonging to the Commonwealth of Nations who wish to improve trade and commerce links to international markets, and are willing to ascribe to a basic Charter that sets out the responsibilities of membership.

It is important to clarify from the start that this is not a reworking of past ideas or arrangements. Those wishing to draw a connection between the earlier works of Joseph Chamberlain or Lionel Curtis may find some affinity with this idea, but not unanimity. The aforementioned individuals formulated their ideas at a time where the British Empire was at its most robust, and where political mechanisms were given as much weight, or even more, than the economic ones. The transformation from Empire to Commonwealth, the political independence and separate development of former colonies, and the examples of international cooperation that allow for economic integration and political sovereignty for nation states, are innovations that could not be adequately addressed by the theories of Chamberlain and Curtis. The idea of establishing an 'Imperial Parliament' would be anachronistic, given the state of the 'Empire' today.

Despite the empirical evidence supporting Commonwealth free trade, the growing trend toward globalization, and the concerns of small to medium sized powers regarding the current geopolitical climate, there is virtually no discussion at present, or existing research on this issue. In many ways, this work is a 21st century revisitation of an idea that has not held much currency for over a half-century. It would not be an exaggeration, therefore, to state that this essay has taken on the ambitious task of initiating and defining a debate that could potentially alter the global economy and shift geopolitical power.[2]

That, however, is not the intent of this work. Such shifts or alterations would, hopefully, assist the development of equal and effective trading relationships within, and outside, the Commonwealth.

Regardless of the direction and eventual outcome of this debate, it is the intention of this work to frame the question as follows – if members of the Commonwealth place importance in that institution; and there are concerns about its relevance into the future; and each member state is committed, either in word or deed, to the notions of economic and political freedom; and there is a genuine concern among those states about an emerging global economy dominated by powerful trading blocs; then why not Commonwealth Free Trade?

While, in the opinion of the author, such a scheme seems to be a logical and self-evident course of direction, the case must, nevertheless, be made. It must also be done with a full recognition of the pitfalls and challenges that would still surface, regardless of the degree of unanimity attained.

---

[2] It is because this work constitutes the beginning of the debate, it will no doubt be surpassed by proponents who will add their intellect and expertise to this enterprise. It shall also be subjected to intense and rigorous criticism and analysis from those who find the scheme to be untenable – in whole or in part.

In discussing the merits of pursuing a Commonwealth Free Trade Association, the case must be made in two respects. First, and most obviously, it must be argued as to whether a CFTA can live up to the expectations; that is, whether or not the plan can make the leap from the theoretical to the practical and do it sufficiently well. Secondly, and just as important, it is necessary to ask why the idea of a CFTA has not been championed or expounded upon until now. If there is so much common ground, and if there are existing relationships that are seen as mutually beneficial, and if there is a generally shared concern about the future of international trade and the growth of regionalism, then why would this suggestion not have been taken up long ago. In short, what is preventing the peoples of the Commonwealth from taking up this idea and seeing it through?

Further to these questions, we will discuss the history of trade within the old British Empire and Commonwealth, the economic resources that Commonwealth nations possess, and would bring to a CFTA, the potential for growth within the CFTA and its impact on global trade in general, the political and strategic benefits of an expanding CFTA, and a proposed governance structure for the organization.

First, under what construct can a Commonwealth Free Trade Agreement be devised? What will be the legal framework of such an agreement? What will it extend to, or include? What will be the responsibilities of participant states? Who will those participant states be? Also, to what extent must a CFTA be involved in issues that go beyond traditional economic considerations?

Beyond particular issues that are specific to Commonwealth states, we must ask what will be the impact beyond a CFTA. How will it affect other economies and societies? Does it offer opportunities for the broader international community? How does it impact existing bilateral and multilateral groupings? How does it contribute to the efforts of the WTO in liberalizing world trade?

This work does not engage heavily into the specifics of an agreement, or the technical issues involved. Should the idea have currency, and be pursued by member states, it will take on the character and complexion of those discussions and negotiations. In a real sense, one could see the creation of a Commonwealth trade zone that owes nothing to what is contained in this book, save for the idea that we must have such a group to begin with. Therefore, one will not find themselves burdened with endless charts, graphs, econometric data, or a treatise on international case law. These important contributions are best left to those who may do them justice.

In truth, one can never fully predict the future should events continue uninterrupted. To forecast it after such a paradigm shift would be beyond the ability of any commentator. In this respect, we are cast in the role of a gambler calculating the odds of winning or losing. A CFTA represents a risk, but in assessing the attributes of the Commonwealth today, and measuring the performance of similar efforts, we can be sure that Commonwealth free trade is a calculated risk.

Discussion of the Commonwealth as a community of nations – where we have been and where we hope to go – is integral to the debate at this stage. Contributing to a globalization that is fair, effective and respectful of people's lives is the guiding philosophy of the Commonwealth of Nations, but it is also the driving force of a Commonwealth Free Trade Association. In the end, it is hoped that those sufficiently intrigued by this idea will be

12

encouraged to develop it further, to shape it, improve it, and give it a life beyond the written word.

*Chapter 2*

WHY COMMONWEALTH FREE TRADE?

For the member states of the Commonwealth, affluent and developing alike, current geopolitical changes present real challenges. Rivalry between the world's two superpowers, the United States and the USSR, meant, to some degree, more influence in the world. Smaller states were often courted to one side or another. The end of the Cold War, and the predominance of the US, leaves these states with little latitude diplomatically. Rather than playing the US against its rival, smaller states compete with one another for access and attention from Washington.

Economically, the US remains the predominant player with the European Union, at present, the only serious challenger. This economic bipolarity, however, does not create the same conditions as the previous East-West rivalry.

It will, by most observers' views, eventually become a multipolar regime, as China, India, Russia, and a reinvigorated Japan take their place. There may also be new trading powers emerge from non-traditional sources. One could, for example, see a nation like Brazil, anchoring a Latin American bloc, move to the forefront in the coming decades.

Under present conditions, however, the world's trade and economic agenda is still defined by an American – European dichotomy. It is the nature of these two actors that must be both understood and taken account of. One power looks outward, but negotiates from a position of strength, and does so only by terms deemed acceptable to its domestic constituency. It can take it, or leave it – and often it does so.

The other power, still emerging, is largely preoccupied with internal and structural matters, and is more focused on expansion within its geographical region. This trend will, no doubt, continue as it attempts to integrate more fully.

The choice for the Commonwealth individually is to gravitate toward one or the other. Turning to Europe means either a polite rebuff, or a minor trade agreement that is limited in scope and effect. Turning toward America often means accepting terms that are only required to meet the litmus test of American decision-makers and their constituents. It is a choice between indifference and the loss of sovereignty.

This is not to suggest that either America or Europe are not suitable partners in trade, or trade liberalization. What it does mean is that as sovereign states broker agreements that are advantageous to their interests, the relative power and influence of one or more of the parties involved decides the quality of the accord reached. That is to say that if there is an inequality in the influence and status of two or more states in a negotiation, the final agreement will, no doubt, reflect this inequity.

If one accepts the status quo as an immutable fact, then little can be done for the prospects of individual Commonwealth nations. If, on the other hand, one entertains the idea that it is a practical possibility to shift this paradigm, then the concept of a CFTA becomes a valid third option.

The Commonwealth of Nations is comprised of over 54 states, possessing over 1/3 of the world's population. It encompasses every habitable region of the world. Its members account for 20 per cent of global trade, and account for 40 per cent of the membership of the World Trade Organization (WTO).[3]

By any theoretical measure – population, human and natural resources, capital, and industrial infrastructure – the Commonwealth is a sleeping economic colossus - the last manifestation of the only truly global empire the world has known in recorded history. Indeed, if one were to have full participation from every Commonwealth member state, and if the average level of GDP per person were more than one-third lower than that of the United States, the valuation of the CFTA economy would exceed US$35 trillion. Combining the GDP's of the United States and the European Union and increasing that figure by half would still fall short of this amount.[4]

According to Mohan Kaul "Thirteen of the world's fastest growing economies are in the Commonwealth and the Commonwealth's understanding of the circumstances and needs of emerging markets is an

---

[3] Commonwealth Business Council – *Enhancing Trade*,
http://www.cbcglobelink.org/cbcglobelink/CBCPage.jsp?headingId=1 (2004 March 18)
[4] All figures based on 1999 World Bank statistics.

important asset."[5] Even in the leading-edge industries of the modern global economy, Commonwealth nations play a prominent role:

> *"Aside from the USA, the leading countries in development of information technology and e-commerce are Commonwealth countries: Australia, Britain, Canada, India, Malaysia, Singapore. Every week, two new Indian software companies open offices in the UK and over 100 Indian software companies are now represented in the UK. The UK is now seen as a gateway to Europe for many businesses, and they are relying on the Commonwealth connection to establish a base and access to that gateway."*[6]

Of course, any predictions are extrapolations based on raw data, and only reflect potential outcomes for a successful agreement. Many other factors will influence the relative levels of economic activity, including: the level of participation of Commonwealth states in an organization, as well as the level of liberalization reached within the final agreement.

When one looks to the results of trade liberalization – in North America, Europe, and elsewhere – one plus one rarely equals two. The efficiencies derived and the freedom to invest and innovate is significant enough to produce results beyond a mere adding of simple numbers. If a CFTA performs to such an extent as to emulate NAFTA, the EU, and the Australia-New Zealand Closer Economic Relations Agreement, we can be assured that there will be a dividend up and beyond the mere adding of economic statistics.

---

[5] Kaul, Mohan , "*The Commonwealth and Globalization*," The Round Table #364 (2002) , p.169
[6] Kaul, Mohan, "*The Commonwealth and Globalization*," The Round Table (2002), 364, p.169

Moreover, as we shall discuss further, possible outcomes are also impacted by the level of development that can be brought to member economies. While opening markets will do a great deal to advance these aims, the creation of a supportive infrastructure must also be part of the discussion. As Gordon Brown points out: "... in the new global economy, neither the United Kingdom, our Commonwealth partners, nor any other country can afford the easy illusion of isolationism. We are all shaped by and must work together to shape the forces at work in our global economy."[7]

While such a situation would hardly transpire immediately, the potential for growth and the creation of wealth certainly justifies further investigation. Even to achieve half of the aforementioned level of development, for example, would make the CFTA the world's largest economic zone.

Members of the Commonwealth share a common language, political and cultural history, as well as governmental organization based on the Westminster model of Parliamentary administration, and the English Common law. There is a history of uniting around common objectives by choice and admitting diversity when compromise is not feasible. It is, in the words of Deryck M. Schreuder, "a working association of independent states – which range from tiny Tuvalu to vast India," adding that "Compared to the United Nations, with its formal international charter, security council, huge bureaucracy and big agencies – including a capacity for military intervention through the deployment of armed forces – the Commonwealth is a relatively informal body which can achieve things informally, as well as by collective action."[8]

---

[7] Brown, Rt. Hon. Gordon, "*New Global Structures for the New Global Age*," The Round Table #349 (1999), p.50

[8] Schreuder, Deryck M., "*A Commonwealth for the 21st Century*," The Round Table #367 (2002), p.651

Whether or not one finds this to be naively optimistic is entirely based on their point of view. The true and unvarnished measure is in whether or not member states find utility in the organization, and see value in being associated with it. As Derek Ingram has observed:

> *"Contrary to most predictions, it not only survives but it grows. It has weathered post-imperial charges of neo-colonialism and acquired a respectability that it is, however inadequately, a force for the global good. Countries with only a slim historical connection aspire to join, and those that left in a fit of pique, misbehaviour or misunderstanding have come back into membership. In 1999 the enormous table in Marlborough House, round which many Commonwealth meetings below summit level are still held, has just had an extra leaf inserted so it can seat all 54 delegates."*[9]

Indeed, as NAFTA and the EU have demonstrated, free trade agreements between states that do not enjoy these common traits have been successful. The EU, in particular, has been somewhat effective in integrating nations with different languages, customs, cultures, political and legal traditions and a history that, within living memory, pitted one against another in deadly conflict.

Advancing the trade liberalization agenda within the context of the Commonwealth of Nations, while not an assured goal, certainly affords some structural advantages both in inception and in its maintenance.

Commonwealth nations, by contrast, not only share the aforementioned characteristics, but, through their membership in that organization,

---

[9] Ingram, Derek, "*A Much-Too-Timid Commonwealth*," The Round Table #351 (1999), p.497

cooperate on a whole host of issues. Among the activities of the Commonwealth Secretariat are:

- The Commonwealth of Learning (COL) which is the only intergovernmental organization in the world dedicated to the development and promotion of distance education and open learning

- The Commonwealth Science Council (CSC), which seeks to promote and build science and technology capacities in both the public and private sectors

- The Commonwealth Fund for Technical Cooperation (CFTC), established in 1971, that provides in-house and external expertise to assist nations in exports, industrial and agricultural development, economic and legal issues, and in developing programs for training and public-sector reform

Harmonizing the economic relations of Commonwealth states, while not an entirely simple affair, provides fewer practical impediments, especially when political integration is not brought into the equation. Indeed, the level of cooperation that exists today provides a solid foundation for such progress.

Building on the already well-established framework of relationships and activities within the Commonwealth, the process of creating a Commonwealth Free Trade Association becomes a less onerous undertaking. What may seem surprising is the fact that leadership within the Commonwealth – political, economic, and social – have not, to date, formulated such a program as it effectively complements existing activities, and – in some respects – enhances their possibility of success. British Prime Minister Tony Blair best made the point when he stated "The Commonwealth should not be reluctant to take on an economic role and an economic profile."[10]

The closest one gets to the letter and spirit of a CFTA is through the activities of the Commonwealth Business Council (CBC). Among its stated objectives are to "encourage trade facilitation and further liberalization of services; encourage developing countries to play an active role in the WTO, and in new trade rounds, by maximizing their negotiating strength through cooperative action; [and] ensure an effective dispute settlement system, recognizing that the Appellate body must be restrained from seeking a supranational role."[11]

The CBC's activities are numerous, to say the least. They include: promoting corporate citizenship and encouraging good governance, expanding e-commerce, mobilizing investment (including public/private partnerships), and influencing public policy.[12] Indeed, if there has been a complaint about the CBC's project, it may be that it has been too timid. Some, like Bishnodat Persaud, argue that the Council should assume more ambitious goals:

> *"It seems to me that the time is ripe for the Commonwealth Business Council (CBC) to take the initiative to get established a trade policy research centre for business. It could be associated with the CBC, but be separately financed. This is suitable for the CBC because it has a good balance of business interests from*

---

[10] Prime Minister's statement to the Commonwealth Business Forum – Wednesday 22 October 1997, http://www.number-10.gov.uk/output/Page1065.asp, September 19, 2003
[11] Commonwealth Business Council – *Enhancing Trade*, http://www.cbc-link.com/cbcnetorg/CBCPage.jsp?headingId=1, September 19, 2003.
[12] Ibid., http://www.cbc-link.com/cbcnetorg/CBCPage.jsp?headingId=1, September 19, 2003.

*developed and developing countries. It could help in the development of a common voice between business in developed and developing countries, and could thus greatly help to promote consensus in the WTO."*[13]

All of the aforementioned activities, and sentiments, run parallel to the goals, objectives, and practical work that would be encompassed within a CFTA. Indeed, if such activities were not currently being conducted, a CFTA Secretariat would be compelled to reproduce them from scratch.

A CFTA would, in fact, provide both additional resources and popular support for the many initiatives that the Commonwealth Secretariat undertakes. This is not to imply or infer that a CFTA would function as part of the Secretariat. Unless the national membership of both organizations becomes interchangeable, one could not presume such a state of affairs. We can, however, assert that whereas freer trade would have a positive impact on the economies of those nations who are net donors to the Secretariat, and that whereas the Secretariat's activities relate to areas of development and cooperation that would help poorer Commonwealth nations qualify for CFTA membership, the activities of both a CFTA and the Secretariat could be independent and complimentary at once.

If one were to view current activities conducted throughout the Commonwealth – formal and informal – one might make the argument that many of the mechanisms of a CFTA exist today. What does not exist, however, are the two elements that would make it a practical reality – a

---

[13] Persaud, Bishnodat, "*Developing Countries and the New Round of Multinational Trade Negotiations*," The Round Table #353 (2000), p.40

schedule to reduce or eliminate tariffs and duties, and a structural mechanism to uphold such an agreement.

Most importantly, in pursuing this modestly activist agenda, the Commonwealth has proven that global actions and multilateralism need not be a threat to national sovereignty. It is a credit to those who have led the organization that it has been able to be effective on issues of mutual concern, and yet has not insisted on assuming supra-national powers to advance its work.

The character of the Commonwealth today reflects the sense of how its members wish to define 'globalization.' In introducing a trade liberalization element to these relationships, it is prudent to be respectful of this historical reality. To conclude an agreement that is successful in its objectives, and remains true to a globalization regime that is more equitable and accessible, it is imperative for us to understand what our alternatives for creating a CFTA are.

*A new globalization?*

In many respects, the current debate on globalization is misleading. To most observers, it appears to be characterized as to whether or not globalization is desirable. This is a false choice. While no precise definition of the term exists, there appears to be a consensus that includes "the intensification of global compression, interdependence, and integration."[14]

---

[14] Hargittai, Eszter and Centeno, Miguel Angel, "*Defining a Global Geography*," American Behavioral Scientist, Vol. 44, No. 10, June 2001, p.1545

That is to say, that "global inhabitants have much more to do with one another and interact more often than they once did."[15] Unless one is arguing that increased interactions among the world's peoples are inherently harmful, this presents a convenient null hypothesis that cannot withstand serious scrutiny.

Globalization is a neutral concept in theory. It is the application of the concept and the consequences of particular choices that make it either positive or negative. The arguments against globalization in its current form centre on the concentration and consolidation of power – political, economic and cultural. While these present valid concerns and points for debate, it is far more useful, and productive, for us to ask how one can develop a globalization model that satisfies these criticisms. The debate, therefore, is not whither globalization, but what kind?

Many commentators see the problem with globalization in its current context as simply 'institutionalizing' the relative position of states, and distributing benefits accordingly. In other words, "states are stratified in complex social, economic, and political arrangements, and the impacts of globalization may well be contingent on where a country is positioned in this system of stratification."[16]

A good example of this phenomenon is presented by Thomas Schott in considering what he refers to as 'global webs of knowledge.'[17] Schott

---

[15] Ibid., p.1545
[16] Sacks, Michael Alan, Ventresca, Marc J., and Uzzi, Brian, "*Global Institutions and Networks: Contingent Change in the Structure of World Trade Advantage, 1965 - 1980*," American Behavioral Scientist, Vol. 44, No. 10, June 2001, p.1580
[17] Schott, Thomas, "*Global Webs of Knowledge – Education, Science, and Technology*," American Behavioral Scientist, Vol. 44, No. 10, June 2001, p.1740

observed the fields of knowledge – education, science, and technology – and how they have been 'institutionalized' by current globalizing trends.

Knowledge, for these purposes, is quantified by such measures as the number of students enrolled in higher education as a percentage of the population, the number of scientific articles authored, and the number of patents obtained by inventors. Applying these measurements to particular nations or regions to the 'global web' should, according to Schott, indicate where the centre, or centres, are, and in what direction does the flow of knowledge take.[18]

What Schott found was that while the United States formed a stable, and relatively self-reliant, centre there has been a steady trend toward 'regionalization.' The European Union, East Asia, and North America are cited as the most notable examples.

These webs of knowledge, however, are heavily influenced by the power relationships existing in the world. As Schott points out "the webs of knowledge are thus not autonomous but are embedded in geopolitical webs."[19] There is a 'globalization' of knowledge webs, but it more often results in extending the influence of the centre than making the whole more cosmopolitan. Plainly put, if the United States is the centre of the web, then globalization is more about American influence on the whole than it is about the whole influencing America.

Specifically, in the realm of science, it means that "the attraction of the center is exerted not only on its surroundings but also within the center

---

[18] Schott, Thomas, "*Global Webs of Knowledge – Education, Science, and Technology,*"p.1742
[19] Schott, Thomas, "*Global Webs of Knowledge – Education, Science, and Technology,*"p.1750

25

itself, and the inwardness of the center has also accumulated and turned into a local parochialism, a 'Not Invented Here' syndrome devaluing foreign cultivation of knowledge and enhancing the value assigned to local knowledge."[20]

This is but a single element in a pattern of global development. In the absence of any structure to global trade – the WTO notwithstanding – the nature of relationships and the flow of influence follow who has the power and how they apply it. A study of this relationship was done by Michael Alan Sacks, Marc J. Ventresca, and Brian Uzzi, as they attempted to determine the level of 'structural autonomy' nations enjoyed in world trade by mapping relationships.

Constraint=0          Primary  Constraint=0          Secondary

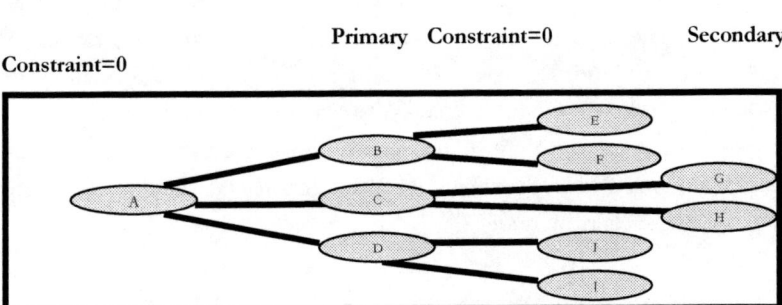

Figure 1: Pure Autonomy (A ; Autonomy =1)

---

[20] Ibid., p.1750

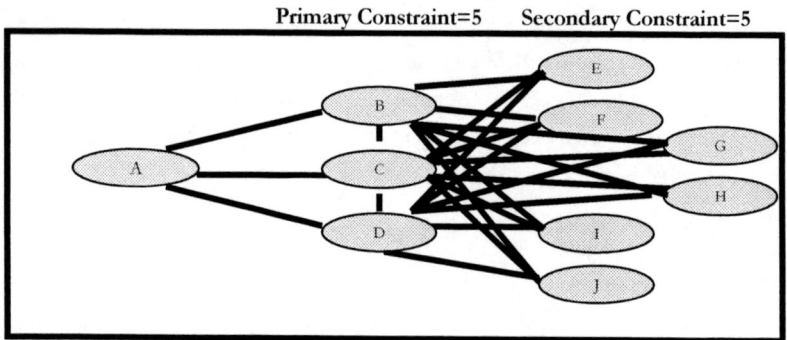

Figure 2: Pure Constraint
(A; Autonomy = 0)

As explained in the first model, Country A has 'pure autonomy' in its dealings because "A has a choice among the three connections for resources, whereas B, C, and D have no alternative to A for information or resources."[21] Also, B, C, and D "have no ability to compare information that A gives them, nor can they collude in any move against A."[22] Under this model, Country A has "relatively more discretion and stand(s) to benefit disproportionately from trade."[23]

Conversely, in the second model, Country A possesses no autonomy in its relationships due to the number of multiple connections among the other players. This means that Country A "cannot play one contact off another, as their connection provides them with information on the actions

---

[21] Sacks, Michael Alan, Ventresca, Marc J., and Uzzi, Brian, "*Global Institutions and Networks: Contingent Change in the Structure of World Trade Advantage, 1965 - 1980*," American Behavioral Scientist, Vol. 44, No. 10, June 2001, p.1583
[22] Ibid, p.1583
[23] Ibid., p.1584

of A on other actors in the network (i.e., pricing, terms of trade, costs, and profits). In short, Country A's "information-gathering and negotiating power has been significantly reduced through the highly constraining nature of the multiple ties within the network."[24]

As a result of developing these statistical models, Sacks, Ventresca, and Uzzi put forth the following propositions concerning the structures of world trade, that:

1. High structural autonomy, or economic independence, will vary directly with the relative wealth of a nation;

2. The more that global trade is structured institutionally, the less effect that such autonomy has on trade;

3. The more countries have somewhat comparable trade regimes, the higher their relative wealth;

4. When global trade is not structured as such, country to country dealings are more associated with wealthier states; and,

5. The relative wealth of a nation dictates the level of benefit.[25]

Simply put, with or without standardized rules of trade, rich nations will benefit. The only difference is that when there are standardized rules, or as

---

[24] Ibid., p.1583
[25] Sacks, Michael Alan, Ventresca, Marc J., and Uzzi, Brian, "*Global Institutions and Networks: Contingent Change in the Structure of World Trade Advantage, 1965 - 1980,*" American Behavioral Scientist, Vol. 44, No. 10, June 2001, p.1587

Sacks, et.al. describe as "global trade institutional structure"[26] less developed players also have an opportunity to benefit.

Globalization, as we have come to know it, has always resembled the 'Pure Autonomy' model. European empires from the 15th century to the mid-20th century built systems where the home country served as the hub of trade and commerce. Colonies of the same power rarely traded with one another without using it as an intermediary.

The British Empire, as we have seen, was no different. Colonies traded directly to Britain, and vice versa, but rarely among themselves. Not only did this place Britain in the position of enjoying pure autonomy, it created an antagonistic relationship between countries like Australia, Canada, New Zealand, and South Africa on matters of trade. Trade between them was marginal and each saw the other as a rival for shares of the British domestic market.

The current global economic regime still is, by and large, a variation on the same theme, with the United States assuming the central role. Over time, however, the only change that appears on the horizon is not a change in structure, but a change in players. The United States will be joined by the European Union, Japan, China, and India – each staking out their particular territory of economic influence.

The closest example of the 'constrained model' would be the internal workings of the EU, where each member state has relatively equal access to institutions and structures. Externally, the EU functions similarly to other

---

[26] Ibid., p.1586

major economic players – as demonstrated by such agreements as the Lomé and Cotonou Conventions. NAFTA is also a more egalitarian model, but the nature of individual side agreements that the US has negotiated with its Canadian and Mexican partners, as well as the power the US enjoys relative to Canada and Mexico, makes it a somewhat skewed example.

For the nations of the Commonwealth, most of which lack the attributes to withstand the pressures and stresses of competing against major economic powers, the status quo institutionalizes their positions.

A Commonwealth Free Trade Association is not a rejection of globalization – but it is a repudiation of the existing architecture. Placing all members on an equal footing allows for a more open and accessible arrangement. It gives countries such as Jamaica and Vanuatu the same legal status as Canada or Britain, eliminating the kinds of structural biases previously discussed. Such equality of status would have little practical effect on the larger industrialized members, but it would constitute a major step forward for smaller states.

The nature of existing agreements outside a CFTA will not change, but what will change would be the resources and abilities that member states can bring to bear. This applies as much to the pursuit of bilateral agreements as it does to collective action through a CFTA. For these reasons, it is of great potential benefit to the member states of the Commonwealth to consider a relationship that allows the free trade of goods and services within a framework that gives each member a full and unimpeded opportunity to develop economically. It also creates an architecture that is not solely dependent upon the economic prospects of one state, as was the case with Britain, and now the United States.

Currently, an economic shock to the US economy would have reverberations throughout the trading world, for that nation is at the centre of many agreements. One need only look to the economic repercussions felt by the nations comprising the 'Sterling Area' after the crisis in the British economy in the mid-1940's – something we will explore in greater detail in subsequent chapters. The design of a CFTA, as we will discuss further, 'spreads the risk' and allows for other trading channels to assume the flows of goods and services should another fail or falter. These alternative channels allow member states the opportunity to engage in market substitution should exports to a particular jurisdiction do not hold.

As we will find, the history of economic and political cooperation, the sharing of common legal and historical legacies, the commonality of interests in a globalizing world, and the superior architecture of a new multilateral trade forum make the case for Commonwealth free trade one worth considering.

*Chapter 3*

THE HISTORY OF EMPIRE & COMMONWEALTH TRADE

Any discussion of the creation of a Commonwealth Free Trade Association must first begin with a discussion of the Commonwealth itself, as well as its precursor, the British Empire. By examining the history of the British Empire in as full a way as possible, we are given a glimpse of two things: the reasons why a Commonwealth Free Trade Agreement is a practical and sensible project; and why many people may be either reluctant, or outwardly hostile, to the idea in the first place.

The Empire consisted of various territories around the world that were either conquered or colonized by Britain from about 1600. Today, most are independent, or ruled by other powers. It reached its apex at the end of World War I, when it encompassed over 25% of the world's population and land area. With a couple of noted exceptions, today's Commonwealth is composed of former and remaining territories of the British Empire.

The British Empire lasted more than three and a half centuries – although it was a relative latecomer. By the time the British began colonizing overseas, the Portuguese and Spaniards had already divided a considerable part of the earth's land surface between them. The Empire grew comparatively quickly, initially with acquisitions in North America and India, as well as some marginal settlement in Africa, throughout the 17th and 18th centuries.

It was during the 1800's when the Empire saw its greatest expansion. Britain acquired many former French possessions in the West Indies, began to settle large numbers in Australia, and competed fiercely with other European powers for territory in Africa. Concurrently, there was a serious expansion in Asia, including the acquisition of Singapore (1824), Hong Kong (1841), Burma (1886), and territories in the South Pacific, including New Zealand (1840).

The final big expansion of the empire was following World War I, when former German and Turkish territories were mandated to Britain and the dominions by the League of Nations, including Iran, Iraq, and Palestine (Israel and the Palestinian territories). Throughout the first two centuries of British Imperial growth, the only serious loss of territory had been the 13 American colonies that formed the United States during the Revolution of 1776.

Commercial interests, rather than territorial ambition, dictated the growth of the early Empire. England in the 16th century was a poor country, lacking the wealth of Portugal and Spain. Early English exploratory efforts were for the purpose of seeking immediate profits. Colonization was, in many ways, seen as a distraction from more important activities. When it did occur, it was often due to the efforts of particular groups, such as the 'Pilgrims' who established the first English settlements in the New England region of the United States.

The early growth of the Empire was not laid down in any coordinated plan and it was held together and administered by whatever means seemed most expedient for a particular time and place. Pirates, traders, soldiers, explorers, financial speculators, missionaries, convicts, and refugees all played a part in creating the British Empire. Private individuals or companies often provided the initial impetus for the exploration and subsequent exploitation of foreign lands, frequently in the face of government reluctance, but, increasingly, British governments were drawn in to maintain them. Perhaps the best-known example of private initiative leading the way was the East India Company. An important exception was in the West Indies, where many members of Parliament had commercial interests and so there was frequent government intervention.

The first successful British colony was Jamestown, Virginia, founded in 1607, although there was an earlier settlement at Newfoundland in 1583. The Empire was gradually built over the next two centuries as the British established colonies and trading posts in many parts of the world, as well as capturing them from other European empire builders. Settlements were made in Gambia and on the Gold Coast of Africa in 1618; in Bermuda in 1609 and other islands of the West Indies; Jamaica was taken from Spain in 1655; in Canada, Acadia (Nova Scotia) was secured from France by the Treaty of Utrecht in 1713, which recognized Newfoundland, Hudson Bay, as well as Gibraltar in Europe, as British. New France (Quebec), Cape Breton

Island, and Prince Edward Island became British territories as a result of the Seven Years' War of 1756-63.

The West Indies was a very attractive target for colonization due to the huge commercial possibilities of the region, mainly the rum and sugar produced there. Between 1623 and 1632, English settlers occupied St Kitts, Barbados, Nevis, Antigua, and Montserrat. Cromwell's forces took Jamaica from the Spaniards in 1655, although it was not officially ceded until 1760, and the tiny Atlantic island of St Helena was annexed in 1673. Belize (British Honduras) was governed as part of Jamaica until 1884.

In North America, the Thirteen Colonies along the Atlantic seaboard between French Canada and Spanish Florida were firmly established by 1733. Colonists had begun to plant cotton in the 17th century, and by the late-18th century it was harvested on a large scale.

This combined with a scattering of settlements in West Africa and the trade from the West Indies to create the 'Triangular Trade': British ships took manufactured goods and spirits to West Africa to exchange them for slaves whom they landed in the West Indies and the southernmost of the Thirteen Colonies. The ships then returned to Britain with cargoes of cotton, rum, sugar, and tobacco, produced mainly by the labour of the slaves.

Following the early settlement in Virginia, British colonies spread up and down the east coast of North America and by 1664, when the English secured New Amsterdam (New York) from the Dutch, there was a continuous fringe of colonies from the present South Carolina in the south to what is now New Hampshire. These colonies, and others formed later, had their own democratic institutions. A dispute regarding taxes, involving the American colonists, roused them to resistance, which came to a head in the American Revolution of 1775-1781 and led to the creation of the United States of America from the thirteen English colonies. The Canadian colonies, however, remained loyal to Britain.

Constitutional development in Canada preceded the events in the United States, with the passage of the Quebec Act of 1775. This was a significant milestone, as it marked the first time that the Parliament at Westminster recognized linguistic, religious, and legal rights that were not recognized anywhere else in the British Empire, including Great Britain itself. These rights included protection of the French language, the Catholic faith, and the legal traditions of the Civil Code. It also preserved the land distribution system of the former French administration.

Following this, and with the influx of refugees from the American Revolution - the United Empire Loyalists – the Royal Proclamation of 1791 which set up New France into two distinct juridical entities - Lower Canada (Quebec), which was mainly French-speaking, and Upper Canada (Ontario), which had an English-speaking majority.

Britain's prosperity was bound up with the slave trade, until it became illegal in 1807. By which time other forms of commerce had become more profitable, and Britain began to emerge as the world's leading industrial nation. In the 19th and early 20th centuries, the Empire made Britain the richest and most powerful nation in the world.

In the War of 1812, the U.S.A. tried unsuccessfully to annex Canada. However, in both the Canadas, there was sufficient discontent to lead to rebellion in 1837. After the suppression of these risings, Lord Durham was sent out to advise on the affairs of British North America; his report, published in 1839, became the basis for the future structure of the Empire.

In accordance with his recommendations, the two Canadas were united in 1840 and given a representative legislative council: the beginning of colonial self-government.

With the British North America Act of 1867, the self-governing dominion of Canada came into existence; to the original union of Ontario, Quebec, New Brunswick, and Nova Scotia were later added further territories until the federal government of the Dominion of Canada controlled all the northern part of the continent except Alaska. Newfoundland, a self-governing dominion through the 1920's, was the last new province of Canada, joining Confederation in 1949.

India was at the heart of the British Empire but it was initially controlled, not directly by the British government, but through the East India Company. This huge company, chartered in 1600, set up a number of factories, as their trading posts were called, and steadily increased its possessions and the territories over which it held treaty rights until its power extended from Aden in Arabia to Penang in Malaya, both vital ports of call for company vessels plying between Britain, India, and China.

The East India Company was the most powerful private company in history, controlling India partly by direct rule and partly by a system of alliances with Indian princes, maintained by the Company's powerful army. The company's political power was ended by the Indian War of Independence (referred to by the ruling British as the 'Indian Mutiny') in 1857. Although this revolt was put down, it resulted in the Crown taking over the Government of India in 1858; Queen Victoria was proclaimed Empress of India on 1 Jan 1877. India then became known as the Indian Empire and the vice-regal representative was called a Viceroy. The British army fought two wars with Afghanistan (1839-41 and 1878-80) to protect

India's northwest frontier and invaded Tibet in 1904. A protectorate existed in Afghanistan from 1880 to 1921. After several years of non-violent protest for home rule from Indian leaders, a semi-Dominion status with a federal parliament was given to India in 1935.

When the Netherlands came under French occupation (1793-1815) the East India Company took the opportunity to occupy parts of the East Indies, such as Ceylon (now Sri Lanka) annexed to the company in 1796. When the British government took over from the company it also acquired the Straits Settlements and by 1914 all Malaya was under British control. Britain gained Hong Kong as a result of the Opium Wars (1839-42) and Kowloon was added to the colony after a second Opium War (1856-58).

Burma (now Myanmar) became a province of British India in 1886 after a series of Anglo-Burmese Wars from 1824. In Borneo, Sarawak was ruled as a personal possession by James Brooke, a former soldier of the East India Company, while the British North Borneo Company acquired Sabah in 1888. The sultanate of Brunei, which had formerly possessed Sarawak and Sabah, itself, came under British protection in the same year.

In Australia, colonization began with the desire to find a place for penal settlement after the loss of the original American colonies. The first shipload of British convicts landed in Australia in 1788 on the site of the future city of Sydney. New South Wales was opened to free settlers in 1819, and in 1853 transportation of convicts was abolished. Before the end of the century five Australian colonies - New South Wales, Western Australia, South Australia, Victoria, Queensland - and the island colony of Tasmania had each achieved self-government; an act of the Imperial Parliament at Westminster created the federal commonwealth of Australia, a self-governing dominion, in 1901. New Zealand, annexed in 1840, was at first a dependency of New South

Wales. It became a separate colony in 1853 and a dominion in 1907. In 1906, an agreement between Britain and France was established for the New Hebrides islands. The German territory of New Guinea was mandated by the League of Nations to Australia in 1919, while the island of Nauru was mandated jointly to Britain, Australia and New Zealand, also in 1919.

The Cape of Good Hope, in South Africa, had been occupied by two English sea captains in 1620, Neither the government nor the East India Company, however, was interested in developing this early settlement into a colony. The Dutch occupied it in 1650, and Cape Town remained a port of call for their East India Company until 1795 when, French revolutionary armies having occupied the Dutch Republic, the British seized it to keep it from the French. Under the Treaty of Paris in 1814, the UK bought Cape Town from the new kingdom of the Netherlands for the equivalent of $6 million. British settlement began in 1824 on the coast of Natal, proclaimed a British colony in 1843.

The need to find new farmland and establish independence from British rule led a body of Boers (Dutch `farmers') from the Cape to make the Great Trek northeast in 1836, to found Transvaal and Orange Free State. Conflict between the British government, which claimed sovereignty over those areas (since the settlers were legally British subjects), and the Boers culminated, after the discovery of gold in the Boer territories, in the South African War of 1899-1902, which brought Transvaal and Orange Free State definitely under British sovereignty. After self-government in 1907, they were merged with Cape Colony and Natal into the Union of South Africa in 1910.

Cecil Rhodes' British South Africa Company, chartered in 1889, extended British influence over Southern Rhodesia (a colony in 1923) and Northern Rhodesia (a protectorate in 1924); with Nyasaland, taken under British protection in 1891, the Rhodesias were formed into a federation (1953-63) with representative government. Uganda was made a British protectorate in 1894. Kenya, formerly a protectorate, became a colony in 1920; certain districts on the coast forming part of the sultan of Zanzibar's dominions remained a protectorate.

The British showed little interest in Africa outside the Cape until the scramble for territory of the 1880s, although a few forts were kept in West Africa, where gold and ivory kept their importance after the slave trade was ended by Britain in 1807. An early exception was the colony of Sierra Leone founded in 1788 with the cession of a strip of land to provide a home for liberated slaves; a protectorate was established over the hinterland in 1896. British influence in Nigeria began through the activities of the National Africa Company (the Royal Niger Company from 1886), which bought Lagos from an African chief in 1861 and steadily extended its hold over the Niger Valley until it surrendered its charter in 1899; in 1900 the two protectorates of North and South Nigeria were proclaimed. World War I ousted Germany from the African continent, and in 1919, under League of Nations mandate, Cameroon and Togoland, in West Africa, was divided between Britain and France.

The high ground of the area made it far more suitable for settlement by white colonists than the colonies in the west. Once again, private companies under charter from the British government pioneered the way, establishing their control over Kenya in 1888 and Uganda in 1890. Somaliland came under direct control of the British government in 1884 and in 1890 Germany, which had already relinquished its interests in Uganda, ceded Zanzibar to Britain in exchange for Heligoland, an island off the German coast. In 1898, after a victorious war against the Mahdi of Sudan, a shared administration between Britain and Egypt was established over the territory, known from then on as the Anglo-Egyptian Sudan. German East Africa was transferred to British administration by League of Nations mandate, and renamed as Tanganyika, in 1919.

The British Empire in the Middle East only lasted for a short time, beginning when the British government bought shares in the Suez Canal in 1856. Britain subsequently occupied Egypt in 1882, declaring it a protectorate in 1914. After the collapse of the Ottoman Empire in 1919, Palestine, Trans-Jordan and Iraq were mandated by the League of Nations to Britain. An uprising against British control in Egypt led to its independence in 1922. British troops, however, continued to guard the Suez Canal until the 1950's. Iraq was also set up as an independent kingdom in 1932. Trans-Jordan gained independence as Jordan in 1946 and the State of Israel was declared in Palestine in 1948.

*Self-government and Dominion status:*

The concept of self-government for some of the colonies was first formulated in Lord Durham's Report on the Affairs of British North America in 1839. It recommended that responsible government (the acceptance by governors-general of the advice of local ministers) should be granted to Upper Canada (Ontario) and Lower Canada (Quebec). Formally adopted in 1841, this blueprint for participatory democracy in British colonies was subsequently applied to the other territories in British North America and to the Australian colonies, which attained responsible government by 1859, except for Western Australia (1890). New Zealand obtained responsible government in 1856 and the Cape Colony in 1872, followed by Natal in 1893.

A further intermediate form of government, dominion status, was devised in the late 19th and early 20th century at a series of Colonial Conferences (renamed Imperial Conferences in 1907). Canada became a dominion in 1867, Australia in 1901, New Zealand in 1907, the Union of South Africa by 1910 and the Irish Free State in 1922. These five self-governing countries were known as Dominions within the British Empire. Their meetings with the British government were the basis for the idea of the Commonwealth of Nations.

Dominion status was very loosely defined until the Statute of Westminster in 1931. From this point, the status of dominion was to be defined as complete self-government. This act was adopted immediately by Canada, the Union of South Africa and the Irish Free State. Australia did not adopt it until 1942, while New Zealand waited until 1947. The Canadian government requested that the British North America Act, which functioned as Canada's constitution, remain in the possession of the British government – the rationale being that the federal and provincial governments could not find a workable consensus for a new amending formula.

A major challenge to the Empire came from Ireland, where it can be argued the British Empire began when Henry II declared himself `Lord of Ireland' in 1171. After 630 years of English rule and 120 years as part of the United Kingdom of Great Britain and Ireland. 26 of the 32 counties of Ireland became the Irish Free State in 1922. The Free State had dominion status but in contrast to the relatively amicable and gradual devolvement of the four other existing dominions, only after centuries of hatred culminating in civil war. A new constitution adopted by the Free State in 1937 dropped the name Irish Free State and declared Ireland (Eire) to be a `sovereign independent state'. The break was completed in 1949 when Eire became a republic outside the Commonwealth, though remaining in a special relationship with the now United Kingdom of Great Britain and Northern Ireland, and becoming a fellow European Union member.

There were varying degrees of unrest throughout much of the Empire during the 1930s, although most notably in India, where Mahatma Gandhi led a campaign of `civil disobedience' against British rule. Muslim League leader Muhammad Ali Jinnah disagreed with the civil disobedience and, fearing a dominance of India by Hindus, began to demand a separate state for Muslims, in areas where they made up a majority. World War II, as we will see, hastened the end of the former colonial empires, mainly because it destroyed the psychological basis upon which their existence depended.

Under the guidance of the last Viceroy, Lord Louis Mountbatten, the British Indian Empire gained independence as the two dominions of India (predominantly Hindu) and Pakistan (predominantly Muslim) in 1947. Mountbatten became the first governor-general of India, and Jinnah became the first governor-general of Pakistan. In 1950 India became a republic but remained a member of the Commonwealth, as did Pakistan in 1956. Burma and Ceylon became independent in 1948. Burma chose to leave the Commonwealth, but Ceylon became a dominion, eventually becoming the Republic of Sri Lanka in 1972, however, remaining a Commonwealth member.

League of Nations mandates were granted to Britain and the dominions in 1919. Those in the Middle East became independent after World War II, but in Africa and Australasia, they became United Nations trusteeships in 1946, continuing under the guidance of Britain and the dominions they were originally awarded to. Most eventually became independent within the Commonwealth after 1960.

Home rule and independence movements began in Africa in the early 1950's, modeled on the movement in India of the 1930's. This started with a home rule campaign led by Kwame Nkrumah in the Gold Coast of West Africa. This resulted in the creation of Ghana, the first independent native-ruled African dominion, in 1957.

Sudan, and Malaya also gained independence in the 1950s. Much of the rest of Africa gained independence in the 1960s, with a majority of the British territories opting to remain within the Commonwealth. Rhodesia declared itself independent in 1965 in order to maintain white minority rule. Britain declared its action illegal, and no other state recognized it, until a final settlement leading to the creation of majority-ruled Zimbabwe in 1980. In the 1970's and early 1980's, most of the West Indies and South Pacific islands had also become independent states within the Commonwealth.

The old dominions, which had stood loyally by Britain's side during World War II, were becoming far more nationalistic in the second half of the 20th Century. Canada was the first dominion to introduce its own citizenship in 1947, as distinct from the common imperial citizenship of British subjects. This was followed by the adoption of a unique Canadian flag in 1965. The last formal constitutional control by Britain was removed in 1982, when Canada finally 'repatriated' its own constitution by introducing a Charter of Rights and Freedoms, as well as an amending formula to the existing British North America Act. Despite ending this last vestige of colonial control, Canada remains a constitutional monarchy, with Queen Elizabeth II being formally recognized as 'Queen of Canada'.

Australian states also had a direct constitutional link with Britain until 1986 when an Australian constitutional Act finally ended this link. A referendum was held on republican status in Australia in 1999, but it was defeated. Thus the Queen remains Sovereign in Australia; also in New Zealand, which maintained very close links with Britain, including a Royal Powers Act, imperial honours and a vast majority of its trade, until after Britain forged closer links with Europe after 1973.

The Union of South Africa adopted a distinctive national flag in 1928 and was transformed into a republic outside the Commonwealth in 1961 after the matter was decided in a referendum the previous year. The mandate over South-West Africa, held since 1919, was terminated in 1990 when it became independent within the Commonwealth as Namibia. The Republic of South Africa also returned to the Commonwealth in 1994 upon the end of apartheid and the election of the first multi-racial government under Nelson Mandela.

By 1973, when Britain entered the EEC, now the European Union, only a few small possessions remained, most of which were proceeding toward independence. Some did not want to end their colonial status. Gibraltar, for example, felt that it risked absorption by Spain if Britain withdrew. Hong Kong was returned to China after the expiry of the 99-year lease over the New Territories in 1997. However, Britain fought a war against Argentina in 1982 to retain control of the Falkland Islands.

*From Empire to Commonwealth:*

From the fifteenth century onwards, a number of territories came within British power at various times by settlement, conquest or cession. The administration of such colonies evolved in different ways to reflect the different circumstances of each territory. The Imperial Conference of 1926, held in London, confirmed the fully autonomous status of the then dominions, including Canada, Australia, New Zealand, the Union of South

Africa, the Irish Free State and Newfoundland. One practical effect was that from this point forward the Governors-General became solely the representatives of the Monarch, and not of the Government of the United Kingdom, as they were before.

In 1931, the Statute of Westminster gave legal form to the new status of the overseas Dominions, removing any remaining restrictions on the legislative autonomy of those realms, except with regard to legislation touching the Succession to the Throne. At that time, it was expected that India would progress towards full self-government, and a semi-dominion status was granted in 1935. Full independence for the territory, as the two dominions of India and Pakistan, was granted on August 15, 1947.

In 1949, to facilitate the desire of India to become a republic within the Commonwealth, King George VI was recognized as 'Head of the Commonwealth', while remaining personal sovereign of those countries within the Commonwealth association who wished to retain a monarchical system of government. It was then that the Commonwealth of Nations took its present-day form.

The British Empire had completely transformed into the Commonwealth of Nations by the late 20th Century. While this process was not without some degree of violence and confrontation, it was achieved in a remarkably orderly process when compared to similar examples in history. Today, there are 54 independent members of the Commonwealth - 16 of which recognize Queen Elizabeth II as Sovereign, five that have their own indigenous monarchies and 33 that are republics.

There are also two almost-independent associated states of New Zealand and 13 remaining British colonies, now referred to as British Overseas

Territories. About 95% of the British Empire remains within the Commonwealth today. Additionally, Mozambique, a former Portuguese colony in southern Africa, and Cameroon, made up mostly of a former French mandate, became members of the Commonwealth in 1995, thus, for the first time, extending the organization beyond the borders of the British Empire. Other aspirant nations, particularly in Africa, are expected to apply to join the Commonwealth in the near future, as it offers many programmes as a stable English-speaking bloc.

*Foundations for the future?:*

Within this historical context, then, the actual idea of a Commonwealth Free Trade Association is neither novel, nor unique. Certainly in the period between 1840 and 1914, free trade existed between Britain and her colonial possessions. As former colonies assumed political independence, and the Empire transformed into the Commonwealth of today, some "Empire Preferential" rules remained until the end of the Second World War. Britain benefited from the system up until the immediate postwar period when the imperial trade legacies became an insulating factor that allowed its industries to fall behind the European peers while still finding semi-captive markets in her former possessions.

That, in itself, is hardly a justification for Commonwealth Free Trade. Indeed, it only attempts to rally people to resurrect economic and political conditions that existed before 1945. It presumes that this period was a time of growth and opportunity for all Commonwealth peoples, and that by simply opening our markets to one another, the standard of living for millions will improve overnight. Such an approach would, at the very least, offend a great number of Commonwealth citizens for whom the past is not remembered with great fondness; at most, it would irreparably undermine a

CFTA from its inception and prevent it from benefiting from hard learned historical lessons.

In asserting the benefits of Commonwealth Free Trade, one must first address the history of the British Empire, both its positive and its negative attributes. One must also make the argument that the last five decades have produced the economic, social and political changes necessary to facilitate a serious consideration of the idea.

First, we must acknowledge that Britain built the largest and richest mercantile empire in human history, and that empire dominated the course of geopolitics from the Napoleonic Era to the end of the Second World War. Historical accounts and statistical data substantiate this posit. Between 1757 and 1947, for example, "British per capita gross domestic product increased in real terms by 347 per cent."[27] As Allister Hinds observed:

> *"Until at least the 1890's...Britain was the richest country in the world. For over a century before the outbreak of World War I, the pound was by far the most important international currency in circulation, and London, the most important financial center."*[28]

---

[27] Ferguson, Niall, *"Empire: The Rise and Demise of the British World Order and the Lessons for Global Power,"* (New York: Basic Books), 2002, p. 216

[28] Allister Hinds, *"Britain's Sterling Colonial Policy and Decolonization, 1939 – 1958,"* (London: Greenwood Press), 2001, p.5

Paul Kennedy found that "...by the period of the Napoleonic War, despite a population less than half that of France, Britain was for the first time ever raising more revenue from taxes each year in absolute terms..."[29]

We may also say that it was a successful endeavor as it accomplished its stated goal – the building of British economic and military power. At the outset of World War I, British interests accounted for 43 percent of all monies invested internationally, 10 percent higher than the combined amount invested by its two main European rivals, France and Germany.[30]

Modern commentators are right to charge that the benefits of the old Empire trading system were not accrued equally, with virtually all wealth being repatriated from the colonies. They are also right to say that the Empire benefited greatly from racially biased policies – from the slave trade to the investment of resources and increasing autonomy in only those colonies where expatriate Britons comprised the largest groups among the local upper and middle classes. These less reputable aspects of Empire are a shameful episode in human history, and should not be understated. Neither should they, however, skew other aspects of the legacy of Empire, many of which provide valuable lessons for today, or foundations for progress.

The old British Empire was a product of its time, and not without coincidence, reflected the degree of enlightenment and social progress of that era. That it did not reflect the social and cultural attitudes of our time may be regrettable, but it is hardly surprising.

---

[29] Kennedy, Paul, "*Rise and Fall of the Great Powers: Economic Change and Military Conflict from 1500 to 2000*," (London: Fontana Press), 1988, p.103
[30] Ibid., p.5

Hindsight is only a benefit to those who view the course of human events as history. It is inevitable, therefore, that future generations will cast a critical gaze on those actions that we, today, find so satisfactory and acceptable.

We must accept that all Empires throughout history have been built with but one objective – to enhance the economic and military power of a state to render it unassailable by its rivals and to maximize benefits to its people – either to the general populace or to its elite. By this measure, we must acknowledge Britain to have been largely successful.

We must also recognize that like the genie let loose from the bottle, individual freedom, democracy and national sovereignty can never be taken away easily. Britain no longer runs an empire, and the other nations of the Commonwealth are no longer colonies or imperial outposts ruled by aristocrats in pith helmets.

Any suggestion that a trade agreement would lead to the resurrection of a quasi-imperial regime fails to take into account not only the practical matters associated with reintroducing the *ancien regime*, but the desire of Commonwealth citizens to do so. It ignores not only five decades of decolonization and nationalist movements, but it places far too low a premium on the aspirations of individuals for political power in society.

Such allegations are, in the opinion of the author, an attempt to dismiss the idea of Commonwealth free trade summarily, or to introduce constructs that are completely superfluous to the issue at hand. Mohan Kaul acknowledges this tendency in asserting that the "modern reality of the Commonwealth is not being successfully projected, particularly in Britain and the old Commonwealth where many people still associate the

Commonwealth with the colonial past. In contrast, in many developing countries, particularly with the younger generation, the first thought is for the opportunities, including business and commerce, which the Commonwealth relationships can offer. The Commonwealth needs to be projected in a modern way, and we need to devote attention to ensure that political leaders convey this message to their people."[31]

Kaul's observation illustrates the benefit of being five decades removed from the days of Empire. It means that the Commonwealth is being inherited by a generation of leaders with no direct or personal experience being colonized. For this generation there has always been home rule, and there has always been a Commonwealth where national leaders stood as equals. The Empire is a remembrance continued by fathers, grandfathers and history textbooks.

This perception allows today's professionals – doctors, lawyers, engineers, among others – to view the Commonwealth more as an informal world community that functions under a language, legal system and political culture that is not alien to their experiences or understanding.

Whether a society chooses to do something, or to do nothing at all, it will not immunize itself from the judgment of posterity. And so, rather than expending effort in trying to elude the inevitable, one may reason that an improvement on the status quo represents a better investment – even if its promise is not necessarily guaranteed.

The true value of history is to instruct us on what works and what does not. Today, at our point in the development of human history, we are called

---

[31] Kaul, Mohan, "*The Commonwealth and Globalization*," The Round Table #364 (2002), p.170

upon to show the wisdom to not repeat our mistakes. One must also show the intellect to recognize what may be good and useful from our past, and to apply it to our mutual benefit today. What is first required is an honest and dispassionate analysis of the facts surrounding the rise and fall of the British mercantile empire.

The weakness of the British Empire was the inherent weakness displayed by every empire throughout history. Once it establishes its dominance, it must continuously fight to preserve that order. Losing the adventurous, risk-taking nature of its creation, it becomes an establishment unto itself, and preservation of the status quo becomes the main preoccupation.

Because of this, other nations, such as Germany and the United States, began to make great strides in industrialization and began to erode Britain's competitive advantage. Unlike Britain, these nations had limited 'formal' empires and were, therefore, freed of many of the costs of colonial administration.

Another constraint on British economic power was the limit to how much domestic consumption could provide demand for goods. While those who lived under British rule accounted for a large percentage of the world's population, many were too poor to purchase goods at any substantive rate. By relying on cheap labour and repatriating profits to Britain, the Empire could only rely on an affluent domestic consumer base smaller than their German and American rivals. Consider the following comparison with Germany:

> "In 1870 the German population had been 39 million to Britain's 31 million. By 1913 the figures were 65 to 46 million. In 1870 Britain's GDP had been 40 per cent higher than Germany's. By 1913, Germany's was 6 per cent bigger than

Britain's, meaning that Germany's average annual growth rate of GDP had been more than half a percentage point higher."[32]

More consumers and a growing middle class meant more demand for products and services, which readily translated into higher rates of growth. The rigid structure of British society very much retarded the creation of a large and affluent middle class, or at least one that was as vibrant as that in German or American society – or even that in the self-governing dominions, like Australia, Canada, and New Zealand. As Kennedy writes "…this position as number one was also the essential British problem. Britain was now a mature state, with a built-in interest in preserving existing arrangements or, at least, in ensuring that things altered slowly and peacefully."[33]

Prior to the outbreak of hostilities in 1914, both Britain and Germany were engaged in a massive buildup of their respective navies, with the German fleet making significant gains against its rival. Also, Germany was actively involved in establishing colonies and trading networks in Africa, becoming a serious competitor to the French, British and Belgians who had dominated that continent for the preceding century.

The First World War created devastation for all nations concerned. The German, Austro-Hungarian, and Ottoman Empires by far suffered the worst consequences of the conflict. It is said, however, that in war there is no victory, just varying degrees of defeat. This adage could have certainly applied to the victorious European powers, including Britain. Victory came

---

[32] Ferguson, Niall, "*Empire: The Rise and Demise of the British World Order and the Lessons for Global Power,*" (New York: Basic Books), 2002, p.295
[33] Kennedy, Paul, "*Rise and Fall of the Great Powers: Economic Change and Military Conflict from 1500 to 2000,*" (London: Fontana Press), 1988, p.298

at an exceptionally high cost in terms of lives lost and the financial price of conducting a new kind of warfare.

The War did not ruin Britain, but it certainly left her anemic. Massive war debts saddled the UK with a drag on the economy at the same moment that her American rival was prospering. Indeed, much of the debt was held by American interests, so the net transfer of wealth was further compounded. As Niall Ferguson points out "paying for the war had led to a tenfold increase in the national debt. Just paying the interest on that debt consumed close to half of total central government spending by the mid-1920's."[34]

In addition to this situation, a return to the gold standard at the pre-war exchange rate created a decade long period of deflationary economic policies.[35] The result was that between 1925 and 1929 Britain's trade declined both in proportion to world trade and in absolute terms, and its balance of payments surpluses did likewise."[36]

### The Ottawa Agreements and the Sterling Area

The onset of the Great Depression did not help matters, and Britain's economy suffered along with the rest of the industrialized world. Between 1929 and 1931 "production in Britain fell and unemployment increased from 10.4 percent to 16.1 percent of the labor force."[37] Despite the devastating

---

[34] Ferguson, Niall, "*Empire: The Rise and Demise of the British World Order and the Lessons for Global Power,*" (New York: Basic Books), 2002, p. 320.

[35] Ferguson, Niall, "*Empire: The Rise and Demise of the British World Order and the Lessons for Global Power,*" p. 321.

[36] Hinds, Allister, "*Britain's Sterling Colonial Policy and Decolonization, 1939 – 1958,*" (London: Greenwood Press), 2001, p.8

[37] Hinds, Allister, "*Britain's Sterling Colonial Policy and Decolonization, 1939 – 1958,*" p.8.

impact of this economic crisis "the significant thing about the Depression in Britain is not that it was so severe but that, compared with its impact in the United States and Germany, it was so mild."[38]

Why would this be the case? Given what we know of Britain's post-War finances, as well as the progress made by the United States as a financial and industrial power, it seems peculiar that Britain would have fared comparatively better. As Ferguson states "what brought about recovery was a redefinition of the economics of Empire."[39]

In 1932, Westminster adopted a policy of "Imperial Preferential" tariffs for colonial products. This had been attempted before, during the Boer War, when Canada was exempted from a temporary duty on wheat and corn exported to Britain. The policy was "to turn the Empire into a Customs Union, with common duties on all imports from outside British territory."[40] The effect was to boost trade in the midst of the worst economic crisis in history. Indeed, "in the 1930's the share of British exports going to the Empire rose from 44 to 48 per cent; the share of her imports coming from there rose from 30 to 39 per cent."[41]

This, incidentally, occurred at a time when the Empire began to decentralize politically – most notably with the Statute of Westminster in 1931, which gave the self-governing dominions like Canada and Australia *de facto* independence from Britain.

---

[38] Ferguson, Niall, "*Empire: The Rise and Demise of the British World Order and the Lessons for Global Power,*" p. 321
[39] Ibid., p. 321.
[40] Ibid., p. 284.
[41] Ibid., p. 321.

The benefit of the Statute of Westminster was that it was the final step necessary to complete the transformation from Empire to Commonwealth. It achieved for the self-governing dominions in the realm of foreign relations what the Durham Report had done for domestic self-determination almost a century before.

While it only applied to the self-governing dominions, it did set a precedent for evolution within the Empire. It acknowledged both the legitimate aspirations to greater practical independence within the context of the Commonwealth, as well as the impracticality of maintaining a centralized imperial power in the 20$^{th}$ century.

For a brief period during the 1930's, Britain and the Commonwealth came the closest it had ever been to the ideals of a CFTA – economic liberalization within the bloc combined with greater political devolution, and more autonomy for the dominions. And as we have seen, it appears to have been a modest success. One might even speculate whether that trend would have continued to fuller fruition had the events of 1939 had not come to pass.

During this time, as well, Britain left the gold standard. Other dependencies, except Canada, and briefly, South Africa, as well as other nations – Ireland, Iceland, the Sudan, Egypt, Iraq and Portugal followed this lead. Together, they formed what became known as the Sterling Area.[42]

The Sterling Area was, at the onset of war in 1939, "formally transformed into a bloc of states, organized by Britain, to protect the value of the pound sterling by maintaining common exchange controls against the rest of the

---

[42] Hinds, Allister, "*Britain's Sterling Colonial Policy and Decolonization, 1939 – 1958,*" p.10

world."[43] As a consequence, fiscal and monetary policy in member countries and in the colonies became tied to the policies of the United Kingdom. This made them "vulnerable to the vicissitudes in the fortunes of the British economy and, inevitably, those of the pound sterling."[44]

## The 'Atlantic Charter' and post-war multilateralism

The coming of the Second World War, however, created the conditions that would set the end of Empire into perpetual motion. The challenge facing Britain was immense – to protect its Empire on all fronts from three major hostile powers, with no help from outside the Empire. At the height of Axis power, Western nations were either conquered, or neutral like the United States and the Soviet Union. Only after sustaining attacks by Japan and Nazi Germany respectively, did those two aforementioned powers join the fight. But in the opening stages of the war, the Empire did effectively stand alone. The choice to fight was, as Ferguson asserts, not a choice at all:

> "By the time Churchill became Prime Minister in 1940, the most likely alternatives to British rule were Hirohito's Greater East Asia Co-Prosperity Sphere, Hitler's Thousand Year Reich and Mussolini's New Rome. Nor could the threat posed by Stalin's Soviet Union be discounted, though until after the Second World War most of his energies were devoted to terrorizing his own subjects. It was the staggering cost of fighting these imperial rivals that ultimately ruined the British Empire. In other words, the Empire was dismantled not because it took up arms for just a few years against far more oppressive empires."[45]

---

[43] Ferguson, Niall, "*Empire: The Rise and Demise of the British World Order and the Lessons for Global Power,*" p.11
[44] Ibid., p.11.
[45] Ferguson, Niall, "*Empire: The Rise and Demise of the British World Order and the Lessons for Global Power,*", p. 296

In order to garner American support, the British government was compelled to agree to conditions that, in many ways, seemed specifically designed to have a deleterious effect on the Empire and its trading system. Specifically, Article VIII of the Atlantic Charter, concluded by Winston Churchill and Franklin D. Roosevelt off the coast of Newfoundland in 1944, explicitly called for an end to imperial preference in the name of a "multilateral, free trade world". Indeed, "If London did not voluntarily fulfill its Article VII obligations as Americans understood them, American officials were prepared to exploit Britain's financial weakness to bring about the end of imperial preference."[46] Indeed, as Niall Ferguson writes "Roosevelt had once joked about 'taking over the British Empire' from its 'broke' masters."[47]

The US strategy regarding the Commonwealth was, in fact, two-fold. While the main negotiations were predicated on capitalizing on Britain's weaknesses, Washington took a "divide and conquer" stance that was designed to draw the individual self-governing dominions – Australia, Canada, New Zealand and South Africa – into separate bilateral arrangements. Using existing free trade legislation that allowed the White House to negotiate limited arrangements without prior Congressional approval, and offering to extend the Mutual Aid Agreement to the dominions, the result was to have the United States supplant Britain as the anchor of the Commonwealth trading system. This, in many ways, truly demarcates the passing of the British Empire, and the ascendancy of a new era of American global leadership.

---

[46] McKenzie, Francine, "*Redefining the Bonds of Commonwealth, 1939 – 1948: The politics of preference*", (Houndmills, Basingstoke, Hampshire: Palgrave Macmillan) 2002., p.38

[47] Ferguson, Niall, "*Empire: The Rise and Demise of the British World Order and the Lessons for Global Power,*" p.346

Why would Commonwealth members willingly agree to this? While the United States was, individually, the world's foremost power, at the end of the war, this did not necessarily have to be the case. Without US leadership in post-war reconstruction, recovery certainly would have taken longer, but it would have happened nonetheless. One could also speculate as to whether a 'Pax Americana' could have ever come into being without the 'help' of Commonwealth states.

The United States, with the exception of Pearl Harbor, did not sustain direct destruction from the war and its infrastructure remained not only intact, but greatly expanded as its industrial capacity turned to rearming Allied armies. This trend was particularly clear in terms of its financial and banking sector, which grew commensurate to America's status as the world's major creditor nation and capital market.

This situation, to a lesser extent however, could apply to Australia, Canada, New Zealand or South Africa. All four dominions escaped the direct devastation of war on their home territory and had their industrial and military infrastructure greatly enhanced by 1945.

A postwar Commonwealth retrenched would give Britain access to the markets she needed for recovery, and would increase demand for dominion products. All of this could have been achieved without bowing to the demands of an American administration that openly stated its goal of dismantling the economic ties within the Commonwealth. Why would this not have been preferable to the course that was eventually taken?

It appears that the American overtures were as well received as they were due in no small part to the internal dynamic of relations within the

Commonwealth. For many years, there had been a growing nationalist movement in each of the dominions – a desire to achieve a greater independence and level of self-determination. While none wished to sever the links to Britain and to each other, they wanted to see the Commonwealth transform from a network of colonies into an association of equals.

More particularly, they wanted decisions to be made by consensus, not by Whitehall. As Lorna Lloyd asserts "The chief impetus behind this change was the dominions' keenness to be formally recognized as Britain's equals rather than its subordinates. It was their right to an equal status rather than a wish to assume international responsibilities that mattered to them."[48]

In the case of Canada, for example, the prevalent strain of nationalism among the English-speaking population from the mid-1800's to the 1920's did not find it inconsistent to be both intensely loyal to the 'Empire,' yet somewhat ambivalent about her relationship with Britain. The sense was that geography, population growth and the rapid pace of industrialization would naturally lead to a situation where the Dominions would surpass the Mother Country in capability, causing a shift in the locus of Imperial power outward to the periphery. In the minds of leading Canadian political thinkers of the day, like Dr. George Grant, it was not simply a question of emulating Great Britain – it was about becoming a "Greater Britain."[49]

Britain's desire to maintain a degree of control over the Commonwealth created an obvious tension, particularly in the ambiguity over the status of the dominions. Lorna Lloyd argues that this was due "partly because of the

---

[48] Lloyd, Lorna, "*Loosening the Apron Strings: The Dominions and Britain in the Interwar Years*," The Round Table (2003), 369, p.280

[49] The author recommends, in particular, the comments of 19th century Canadian author Stephen Leacock with reference to Canada's perceived role in the Empire, and its aspirations thereof.

conceptual fog that surrounded their status, which in turn was partly a reflection of Britain's pragmatism. This approach helped Britain to avoid facing the full implications of the growing stature of the dominions. It wanted to keep them tied to its apron strings, to bolster both its reputation and its power. While not obstructive of dominion ambitions outright, Britain did not encourage them. It made concessions when they were necessary but pretended to itself and to the world that, at bottom, nothing had changed."[50]

To characterize the actions of the dominions as some form of backlash against British control, however, would be unfair. From a practical standpoint, there were some practical considerations that enticed them into the US camp. For dominion governments seeking to achieve a greater degree of independence, the American proposal of a multilateral framework, including access to American markets, was appealing.

While each of the dominions had significant trade with Britain, they did very little trade between each other. A loss of the Australian market to Canada, and vice versa, would have mattered very little. Indeed, in many ways, the dominions saw each other not as partners, but as rivals, as each was focused on competing for market share within Britain. Now their largest market was on the verge of financial collapse, and was conceding imperial preference to assuage the new economic powerhouse of the world, the United States, who, in turn, offered them bilateral agreements, and a commitment to a new regime where they would be considered as equals. After the sacrifices of war, and the unreliable nature of the status quo, it was too tempting an offer to pass on.

---

[50] Lloyd, Lorna, "*Loosening the Apron Strings: The Dominions and Britain in the Interwar Years*," The Round Table (2003), 369, p.279

Britain and the rest of the Sterling Area were to get a sense of what was to come on July 15, 1947 – the day that the UK, in fulfilling its terms of postwar agreements with the United States, officially made the pound sterling convertible with other currencies. Immediately, the move sent shockwaves throughout the Commonwealth trading system. The British government rescinded the move only after five weeks, but the damage was done. Unfortunately, by attempting to contain the fallout, this reversal drew the ire of the United States, who promptly put much of the GATT agenda on hold.

For members of the Sterling Area, action was needed to address the depleted gold and dollar reserves that, by backing the pound, backed their own currencies, through a system of reserve-pooling. As a result, Britain, Australia and New Zealand cut their dollar imports in order to preserve their position. The only exception was Canada, as it was not a member of the sterling area. Despite benefiting from being part of the dollar area, the tariff preferences Canada had with other Commonwealth states were seriously devalued as "in a world of dollar licensing and currency restrictions these trading privileges were virtually useless."[51]

A larger issue that helped hasten the end of the Sterling Area, and the broader project of Commonwealth trade, was the comparative status of the UK to its Dominion partners. While Britain was heavily in debt, Australia, Canada, New Zealand, South Africa, India and Pakistan all had opportunity to accumulate cash reserves. Britain's only option was to focus on developing resources within her colonies, but even this was sacrificed in the name of preserving the Sterling Area. Within the decade, even this resource

---

[51] Rooth, Tim, *"Economic Tensions and Conflict in the Commonwealth, 1945 – c.1951,"* Twentieth Century British History, Vol. 13, No. 2, 2002, p.125

was in doubt, as British colonies were pursuing the goal of independence and statehood.

As we can see, the collapse of the old British mercantile empire was the result of many factors, including: the loss of competitive advantage over its rivals, the lack of development of an economic middle class in many of its colonies, the financial impact of the First World War and the Depression, the trend toward protectionism, the Second World War and the Atlantic Charter with the United States, as well as the postwar agreements that led to the 'dollarization' of currencies and the pressure toward decolonization.

In many ways, two global wars, depression, and the rising levels of competition from outside the Empire converged in what could be considered as a geopolitical 'perfect storm.'

*A future in Europe?:*

The final act was the decision for Britain to join the European Economic Community (EEC) in 1973. Prior to this, and despite the other contributing events, the Commonwealth remained the cornerstone of British overseas trade:

*"It is true the proportion of British trade with the countries that formed the EEC grew from 12 to 18 per cent between 1952 and 1965. But the share of total trade with the Commonwealth remained substantially larger: though it fell from 45 per cent to 35 per cent, it remained twice as important as EEC trade....It was only after British entry into the 'Common Market' that European protectionist tariffs, particularly on agricultural products, forced a dramatic reorientation of British*

*trade from the Commonwealth to the continent. As so often, it was the political decision that caused the economic change, not the other way round.*"[52]

In the intervening three decades, Britain has adjusted to this new European-oriented economic relationship. Today, trade with Commonwealth nations still amount to a significant portion of UK overseas trade. It does, however, pale in comparison with the amounts traded with the United States and within the EU.

As the EU continues to expand its borders eastward and it works steadily toward creating the institutions indicative of a federal state structure, this trend will only increase in its scope and impact. Whether or not Britain is reconciled with the bigger project of political harmonization is a source of much debate in that nation. As that debate develops, and the positions become more sophisticated, it may be evident that Britain can reconcile commitments to both the Commonwealth and Europe.

While the absence of Britain within a CFTA would be regrettable and significant, it need not present an insurmountable challenge to its formation. The creation and full functioning of a CFTA may be a prerequisite for later participation, as we will discuss later at further length.

This brings us to the present, a world where, despite a universal commitment to freer trade and open markets, prosperity for nations is determined by the level of access one has to markets, namely mature and developed ones.

---

[52] Ferguson, Niall, "*Empire: The Rise and Demise of the British World Order and the Lessons for Global Power,*"p. 354.

## *Time for Commonwealth free trade?:*

As we have seen, many factors – and not all economic in nature – contributed to the decline and erosion of the old Imperial trading system. This, however, does not necessarily preclude the existence of a new, more democratic, less centralized regime. Indeed, it is through a careful and objective study of previous efforts that we can see what must be done, or avoided, in the structuring of a new trading framework.

Dramatic and revolutionary changes to the geopolitical status quo created a 'perfect storm', which sank the British Empire. Such a convergence of events and circumstances is rare indeed, and it is highly doubtful that we may see a parallel situation occur. Moreover, a desire to preserve a paternalistic relationship between Britain and the dominions undermined any attempt to build a superstructure that would not only encourage trade between the UK and other Commonwealth states, but also promote the growth of trade linkages throughout a CFTA zone.

Indeed, rather than a return to the days of Empire, a CFTA provides the best possible opportunity to preserve the independence and integrity of nation-states.

The choices are to enter into bilateral agreements with powerful nations determined to dominate and shape the agenda, to place one's faith in multilateral negotiations with the backing of ad hoc coalitions vulnerable to fragmentation, or in a free trade organization where each nation-state is equal in stature, and where the rules of conduct are well known and understood.

Ideally, a CFTA should fulfill the following criteria, as suggested by David French in his examination of the Commonwealth Institute:

*"Business people understand the benefits of investing in stable, outward-looking countries that share language, legal systems and economic approach. The business arm of our plan has its genesis in our belief that there is a strong but sometimes unseen network of business interests in the Commonwealth: companies do business with each other across the Commonwealth but frequently ignore the Commonwealth dimension. We hope to contribute to raising the profile of the Commonwealth in these business networks, and stimulate their growth as a result."*[53]

It is in the spirit of this sentiment that we discuss the possibility of formalizing existing relationships for the benefit of the Commonwealth as a whole.

---

[53] French, David, "*Rethinking the Commonwealth Institute*," The Round Table #352 (1999), p.662

*Chapter 4*

OBJECTIVES OF A CFTA

The best means to describe what the objectives of a CFTA are is to assess what is the challenge that needs to be met. Expression of this can be found in the text of the Fancourt Declaration on Globalization and People-Centred Development, endorsed by Commonwealth leaders' meeting in South Africa in November, 1999.[54]

The Declaration opens by stating that "in today's world, no country is untouched by the forces of globalization. Our destinies are linked together as

---

[54] see Appendix J, p.

never before. The challenge is to seize the opportunities opened up by globalization while minimizing its risks."[55]

In terms of specific remedies, Commonwealth leaders expressed a desire to see movement on improved market access for exports from developing countries, opportunities for those states to build up their skills base and manufacturing capabilities, upholding labour standards, and environmental protections.

Moreover, it also called for action on national debt burdens, development of civil society, greater transparency and accountability, the rule of law, and the elimination of corruption in both private and public life.

It is important to bear in mind that these recommendations are compatible with – and in some respects, synonymous with – the basic processes recommended for the structure of a CFTA. Also, we must remember that the potential membership of a trade agreement would be comprised of nations who have already lent their agreement to its principles in the guise of Fancourt. In this respect, any agreement should be considered as a natural progression of trends and initiatives being undertaken by the Commonwealth's membership – both formally and informally.

A CFTA, by its very design, would place all member states on an equal footing. Its organizational structure would enshrine the principle of equality of status for all member states, regardless of size of population, territory or economy. Issues of competitive advantage and the growth of an economic middle class would remain within the ability of member states to address through their respective sovereign national governments. Success or failure

---

[55] Ibid..

in this regard will hinge on the ability of those national governments to respond to the needs of their own people, and not a centralized supranational bureaucracy.

The CFTA's single objective is the reduction, and eventual elimination, of tariffs and duties between member states. It also includes the eventual elimination of corporate regulations pertaining to ownership and operation between member jurisdictions. CFTA states would still maintain the right to legislate on issues of corporate conduct, including ethics, environmental protections, labour standards, and taxation. Practically, the CFTA would limit itself to eliminating national barriers to investment, ownership, and conduct within the domestic markets of member nations.

An example would be the case of banking. A British bank like Barclays, for example, would be free to conduct business within Canada as if it were a Canadian bank, with no added restrictions. The Canadian operations of a British bank, however, would fall under the jurisdiction of Canada's Bank Act in the same way as Scotiabank, or the Bank of Montreal would be regulated domestically. CFTA members would, in effect, treat enterprises from other member states as domestic concerns, with no added "foreign" regulation, but fully required to abide by the laws and regulations of the respective host nation. This, of course, is a standard component of bilateral and multilateral trade agreements, that 'national treatment' would be extended to corporations based in a partner state.

Indeed, the practical economic scope of a CFTA would be to reduce, or eliminate, tariffs and duties existing between its members, and to remove regulations that would have CFTA-based enterprises treated as foreign entities. The actual scope of the agreement need not extend beyond this territory to be considered effective.

In this way, member states will enjoy the benefits that trade liberalization will bring, while preserving the sovereignty of the nation state, which is the cornerstone of democracy and public accountability.

CFTA member states, through their elected governments, may choose to enact laws that fulfill a policy or development agenda – whether it is the promotion of linguistic or cultural programs, or plans designed to address regional disparities.

Again, nothing impedes a nation-state from carrying out such schemes. The CFTA, however, does require that insofar as the private sector may be involved, either through activity in that area, or in the bidding for government contracts, that CFTA-based enterprises enjoy a domestic status.

For example, it may be decided by a British or Australian retailer to establish operations in Canada, Quebec in particular. That province, in order to safeguard and promote the French language, requires retailers to comply with language laws. CFTA enterprises would have the right to participate under those rules just as the government has the right to pass them.

Should a CFTA member deem it a national government priority to enact rules that are designed to protect cultural heritages, enterprises from throughout the CFTA would be free to participate in broadcasting, publishing, or other cultural endeavours under the condition that their activities in that particular jurisdiction are fully compliant with national standards. If, as an illustration, South African law required a particular percentage of media programming be made available in either the Xhosa or Zulu languages, British, Australian, or Canadian broadcasters could offer it under those conditions. Conversely, South African content producers may be free to offer French-language products for Quebec, or Scots Gaelic for Scotland.

In particular, this creates an incentive for producers in the developing Commonwealth. To profit from sales to the more affluent nation-states of a CFTA, those enterprises will need to comply with the health, safety, and cultural standards of the nation that receives those imports. Also, where local governments have put into place particular environmental regulations, industry will be compelled to comply.

Some critics may be quick to charge that some jurisdictions will be more lax in their application of environmental standards. They would argue that a CFTA must have a binding agreement on standards, with a monitoring schedule and penalties for non-compliance.

There are reasons, however, for not pursuing this direction. First, one must be prepared to presume that a CFTA is, indeed, a supra-state structure, for it will exercise authority over and beyond its role as a trade liberalization organization. Also, there already exists a great number of domestic laws within Commonwealth states, as well as international treaties and conventions that compel environmental stewardship. Adding another authoritative body will not produce better results, but it will substantiate the need for restrictive rules and bureaucratic oversight. Finally, one could make the case that the general conduct of CFTA affairs will lead to improvements.

Poorer nations entering the CFTA will, first and foremost, focus their work on infrastructure – schools, hospitals, transportation and communications. This new infrastructure, however, will enjoy modern technology, which tends to be more efficient in resource use, more productive, and leaves a smaller 'footprint' than some of the older facilities in Europe and North America.

We must also acknowledge the role of public opinion in moving the agenda. Already there is a growing constituency among consumers who are interested in letting their social conscience guide their choices. Whether it be investing in 'ethical' mutual funds, or only purchasing 'fair trade' products, the power of consumers compels producers and manufacturers to respond positively.

One possible compromise could be a policy of linking standards, similar to the concept behind the "Sullivan Principles" adopted by US companies doing business in South Africa during the latter part of that country's apartheid era. It required those enterprises to treat their South African employees similarly to workers in the United States.

By this notion, Canadian, British, Australian, and New Zealand corporations would be mandated to enact employment standards equal to those of their home government. This would mean that these enterprises would meet, and almost certainly exceed local standards in areas such as wages and benefits, workplace health and safety, training and skills development, as well as collective bargaining.

Some may argue that for producers, this negates any advantage in producing through operations overseas. This, however, primarily impacts the labour cost differential, which, it can be argued, is only part of the calculus. Manufacturing efficiencies and infrastructure quality are just as vital. Moreover, wage inflation, up to a point, helps to nurture the creation and growth of a consuming middle class. This, in turn, develops an indigenous market that would provide opportunities for domestic and CFTA-based enterprises alike.

Lastly, it has already been established that the CFTA will only grant membership to those nations that observe the provisions of its Charter. When one guarantees basic and fundamental principles of liberty and democracy, people are given the power to assert their interests. It is rational to assume that any people who are endowed with education and opportunity, guaranteed by freedom and true democracy, would be unwilling to accept conditions that would harm them, their loved ones, and the broader community.

What the CFTA must do is to find the optimum balance point between economic integration and political autonomy. While no one legitimately believes that such an agreement can work with no compromises or any degree of harmonization, the starting point of discussions should also be the only point. That is, what is absolutely necessary to facilitate economic progress. Economics, not political institution-building, must remain the enduring focus.

Chapter 5

ECONOMIC OPPORTUNITIES FOR A CFTA

In order to establish the parameters of Commonwealth Free Trade, and the potential for such an organization, it is important for us to look at what assets the Commonwealth possesses today, and what the implications of freer trade would mean for their growth and expansion. For the purposes of this analysis, we will identify the Commonwealth as a single entity.

The Commonwealth of Nations is currently comprised of 53 nations, territories and dependencies. While the membership of the Commonwealth is essentially based on the former territories of the British Empire, it is not exclusively the case. Mozambique, a recent addition to the organization, had been previously under Portuguese control. Also, several other nations have floated the notion of Commonwealth membership – including, oddly enough, both the State of Israel and the Palestinian Authority.

While we do not know what a fully engaged CFTA would represent, we can measure the aggregate of its constituent parts. It is because the level of trading transactions between Commonwealth states – with some noted exceptions – tends to be low; a CFTA would represent a measurable expansion of commerce for each member. Therefore, we can safely presume because of this, and the measured impact of similar agreements, that these figures will represent minimum levels. As with all trade agreements, the synergies achieved between economic actors create their own dynamic.

Economic activity is impacted by many variables, both market-related and regulatory. The latter represents a category that is, in essence, difficult to define. It hinges on several factors, including political and bureaucratic decisions, community standards, as well as limitations imposed by geography and the environment. Because local standards and physical realities set the pace, it is exceedingly difficult to offer anything more than a cursory picture of basic practices, as would be proscribed in a CFTA Charter – political and economic liberalization, observance of human rights, and such.

In terms of tangible market inputs, there are also many factors to measure, but we may attempt to do so as these categories are easily translatable into any of the possible contexts we would find among jurisdictions. These relate to the value of national economies, levels of industrial outputs, the amount of available capital, the vitality and relative maturity of private economic actors, as well as the availability of resources – human and natural.

## GDP

Currently, the aggregate population of the Commonwealth is approximately 1.84 billion persons, with a Gross Domestic Product (GDP) of US$3.51 trillion. This, however, only translates to a per capita GDP of US$4615 – fully one-fifth that of Australia, Canada, New Zealand or the United Kingdom. Indeed, if the Commonwealth were to develop to the standard of its wealthiest members, at a per capita GDP of US$21,000, then the aggregated Commonwealth economy would be US$38.7 trillion. This compares to the United States at around US$11 trillion, and the European Union at US$8.5 trillion.

**Economic Statistics (by selected countries), 2001**[56]

| Country | GDP ($US million) | GDP per capita ($US) | Real Growth (%) | Inflation (%) |
|---|---|---|---|---|
| Australia | 465,900 | 24,000 | 2.3 | 4.3 |
| Bangladesh | 230,000 | 1,750 | 5.6 | 5.8 |
| Canada | 875,000 | 27,700 | 1.9 | 2.8 |
| India | 2,500,000 | 2,500 | 5.0 | 3.5 |
| Mozambique | 17,500 | 900 | 9.2 | 10 |
| New Zealand | 75,400 | 19,500 | 3.1 | 2.6 |
| Sierra Leone | 2,700 | 500 | 3.0 | 15.0 |
| UK | 1,470,000 | 24,700 | 2.4 | 2.8 |

---

[56] Source: U.S. Census Bureau, *International Database and The World Factbook*, 2002

If we were, however, to restrict our survey to the four largest industrialized members – Australia, Canada, New Zealand and the United Kingdom – the aggregated GDP would be in excess of US$2.8 trillion.[57]

*Foreign Direct Investment*

While there are many factors that impact foreign direct investment, it can really be considered a measure of two things: one, the vibrancy of a national economy; and second, the confidence that investors have in the institutional structures that support it. It is no secret that investors are risk-adverse, and are attracted to areas where they can be assured a respectable rate of return on their original resource outlay.

**Foreign direct investment, net inflows (BoP, current $US million)**[58]

| Country | 2002 |
|---|---|
| Australia | 16622.4 |
| Canada | 20501.3 |
| New Zealand | 823.1 |
| UK | 28180.2 |

The "Big Four" drew in, in 2002, a combined US$ 66.1 billion, in foreign direct investment. While there would be a particular amount of this that would be attributed to cross-investment among the aforementioned countries, it would be accurate to state that the largest amount of this total

---

[57] Source: World Bank, *World Development Indicators database*, www.worldbank.org, 2004 Aug 16
[58] Source: World Bank, *World Development Indicators database*, www.worldbank.org

would come from outside sources, particularly outside the Commonwealth, which, by definition, means sources outside a proposed CFTA. The Canadian total, for example, is heavily affected by cash inflows from the United States, while the British amount would be reflective of sources from within the European Union.

Notwithstanding these figures, leading economies within the developing Commonwealth have also attracted a great deal of capital. Singapore, for example, attracted over US$6 billion in 2002, while India and Malaysia each garnered over US$3 billion.[59]

Trade liberalization within the Commonwealth, based on a programme that combines political and economic reforms with the preservation of local sovereignty, should only serve to increase these figures. This, in turn, will help the developing partners within a CFTA develop and build the infrastructure necessary for an eventual transition to developed status, while the developed partners will benefit from the opportunities that come from building larger, more comprehensive financial and capital markets. Moreover, these economies will be able to attract even more capital, as economic actors in non-CFTA states are attracted to new investment opportunities.

*Natural Resources*

To fully account for the natural resources available within the Commonwealth, one would readily find every raw material necessary to facilitate modern manufacturing and industrial output. Commonwealth nations figure prominently among those with the world's largest reserves of

---

[59] Source: World Bank, *World Development Indicators database*, www.worldbank.org

precious metals and gemstones, iron ore, oil and natural gas. Many member states, being among the most industrialized nations in the world, also possess the facilities and the technical know-how to convert these resources into products ready for consumption.

Of primary note, nations like Australia, Canada, Nigeria, and South Africa enjoy an abundance of raw minerals – from precious metals to industrial ores to renewables. In terms of oil and gas resources alone, Nigeria is a major OPEC producer, while the Athabaska Tar Sands of northern Alberta, Canada are estimated to hold the equivalent of approximately 1.6 trillion barrels of oil – roughly equal to half the world's known supply of conventional deposits.[60]

Beyond this, Commonwealth resource companies are among the largest players in the resource sector. Corporations such as BHP Billiton, Anglo American, Alcan, BP and Royal Dutch Shell are recognizable as global leaders in their milieu. The following table represents aggregate values for Commonwealth companies in particular resource industries, drawn from Forbes' Magazine's Global 2000 list:

| Industry | Sales* | Assets* | Market Value* |
|---|---|---|---|
| Chemicals | 22.91 | 25.81 | 20.49 |
| Materials | 139.23 | 231.35 | 268.80 |
| Oil and Gas operations | 492.51 | 468.59 | n/a |

[60] "*Athabasca Tar Sands*" – The Free Dictionary, http://encyclopedia.thefreedictionary.com/Athabasca%20Tar%20Sands, 2004 September 20.

*Agriculture*

In terms of agriculture, Canada, Australia, New Zealand, South Africa and Malaysia are members of the Cairns Group, representing net exporters of food products. In addition, other smaller Commonwealth states, while not wholly self-sufficient in food production, do harvest particular and unique products that have ready markets worldwide.

In terms of agrifood production, the aggregate market value of Commonwealth businesses in that industry sits at roughly US$253 billion, with assets of US$204 billion, and sales exceeding US$164 billion.[61]

As far as agricultural output is concerned, if one restricted the sample to only those Commonwealth nations that still retain H.M. Queen Elizabeth II as their Head of State[62], based on 1992 data, this group would account for 2.4 per cent of rye production and 4.5 per cent of the world's supply of wheat.

*Capital and Financial Services*

Access to capital and investment resources is vital to economic growth and expansion. Stock markets in London and Toronto rank among the ten largest in terms of capitalization, while stock exchanges in Sydney and Johannesburg are important markets for specific regions and sectors. In adding the market capitalization of the three aforementioned exchanges, only the New York Exchange would exceed it. Indeed, the combined amount is

---

[61] Forbes.com, Global 2000 ranking database, www.forbes.com, 2004 Aug 16
[62] Antigua & Barbuda, Australia, Bahamas, Barbados, Belize, Canada, United Kingdom, Grenada, Jamaica, New Zealand, Papua New Guinea, St. Kitts & Nevis, St. Lucia, St. Vincent & Grenadines, Solomon Islands, Tuvalu, and their respective territories.

larger than the Tokyo Exchange, and is roughly equivalent to the high-tech NASDAQ.[63] In addition, markets in emerging economies such as India offer investors great opportunities for high growth returns.

### Major Commonwealth Stock Markets[64]

| Market / Exchange | Average daily volume (shares) | Capitalization (in US$) |
|---|---|---|
| London | 2.1 million | $2.8 trillion |
| Toronto | 197.5 million | $1.7 trillion |
| Sydney | 1.02 billion | $370 billion |

<u>Banking and Financial Services</u>

In terms of banking and financial services, Commonwealth-based enterprises are prominent in the global economy. In 2004, the aggregate assets of the largest of the Commonwealth-based enterprises were as follows[65]:

| Industry | Sales* | Assets* | Market Value* |
|---|---|---|---|
| Banking | 348.25 | 6128.28 | 790.08 |
| Diversified financials | 63.62 | 348.05 | 96.07 |
| Insurance | 251.86 | 1333.72 | 176.10 |

* all figures expressed in US$ billions

---

[63] http://investsmart.coe.uga.edu/C001759/world/world_nf.htm, 2004 June 18
[64] http://investsmart.coe.uga.edu/C001759/world/world_nf.htm, 2004 June 18
[65] Forbes.com, *Global 2000 ranking database*, www.forbes.com, 2004 August 16

Based on these figures, the combined assets of the largest enterprises within these three categories stand at US$7.8 trillion – almost the equivalent of the GDP of the European Union prior to the membership expansion in 2004. When one also includes smaller players, whether they are national or regional – one could easily see this number increase to a level where it closely approximates the GDP of the United States.

The relative status of this industry is vitally important. It provides the capital which is the lifeblood of private-sector enterprises, the asset management capabilities necessary for upper- and middle-class families to build their own personal holdings, and the taxation revenue for governments to reinvest in social development and assistance programs for poor and low-income individuals.

As many of the prospective members of a CFTA lack a fully developed domestic financial services infrastructure, access to these actors will ensure that development can occur at virtually every level of economic activity. Businesses will be able to secure financing for expansion and acquisitions, while private individuals will have access to secure consumer borrowing and private asset management tools from the beginning. Moreover, local concerns will benefit from this activity in two respects: first, as per capita incomes increase, so too, will the demand for their services, whether it be in regular deposits or investment accounts; secondly, they will enjoy the same market access as larger players, and will be free to expand to other CFTA markets. Indeed, as their asset base increases, they will be able to offer more services and be more competitive in both the domestic and international markets, both within and outside the CFTA.

Also, it is important to consider Commonwealth-based private-sector enterprises as an asset in themselves. Not only are they the best vehicle for investment, industrialization and investment, they are also vital to an economy insofar as their profits and payment of dividends enhance GDP and allow for even more investment capital for growth and expansion. Commonwealth-based companies are prominent among the largest, most advanced and competitive in the world in many sectors – banking, insurance and financial services, aerospace, engineering, petrochemicals and refining, agrifood, media and broadcasting, computing and other technologies.

While much focus is given to the benefits to access to developed nations, it is also important to reflect upon the opportunities available in developing nations that would be part of a CFTA.

Engineering firms, for example, would find opportunities in work related to building infrastructure, including roads and highways, airports, rail links and shipping terminals, water and sewage treatment facilities, and electrical grids. Moreover, more specialized firms would be able to supply physical support or consulting for the provision of specialized services, such as health care, education, civil engineering, and administrative functions.

The building of industrial capacity in the developing world affords the host country a 'launch pad' for further economic growth and expansion. For the developed partners, it means new customers, new markets, and new opportunities for investment and growth in their own right. For both, it means an economic relationship that is stable, predictable, respectful of democracy, and responsive to the business community.

A common language and legal tradition also allow for a greater degree of cooperation and coordination. The Commonwealth Business Council, for example, believes that "that a shared language (English is the first or second language throughout the Commonwealth), common-law tradition and accounting conventions deliver a "10-15% increase in efficiency in dealing with [other] Commonwealth [members]".[66]

A logical expectation by all of this is to create an environment within a CFTA where average growth rates are higher than those of the G8 nations over the past decade. Sustained rates of growth that combine the 2 to 3 per cent of Canada with the 6 to 7 percent of India, for example, would provide across the board growth that, in turn, secures the promise of further economic expansion. This, of course, shows the challenge for both sides. The industrialized world possesses the capital and the know-how, but lacks the kind of opportunities for growth and expansion seen in the developing world. Developing nations, conversely, provide great opportunities for significant and substantial growth, but lack the capital and the infrastructure to turn this potential to their advantage.

Although no one could accurately assess what the cumulative effect of such trade liberalization would be on the economies of the Commonwealth, and given that in similar circumstances some domestic industries have undergone difficult transformations, the experience of other regimes would point to a significant increase in transjurisdictional trade and steady increases in GDP. Such has been the experience of the Canada-US agreement, as well as the CER treaty between Australia and New Zealand. When one considers the preconditions for a CFTA, as well as the practical conduct of its economic partners, these examples are the most relevant and the most instructive.

One may concede that the economic impact of a Commonwealth Free Trade Association can only be estimated in terms of scope. It is fair to

---

[66] Economist. Com, "*What's the Commonwealth For?*", Global Agenda London: Dec 8, 2003. pg. 1

surmise from existing data, and the experiences of trade liberalization since the end of World War II, however, that where nations have concluded reciprocal agreements, there has been noticeable growth in national GDP as well as measurable net growth in employment opportunities. And while one adverse effect may be the sectoral dislocations and job losses in particular sectors, should a CFTA be concluded in such a way as to not impede national governments in setting local standards, they will be free to devise programs and policies to address those pressing concerns.

Chapter 6

THE LOMÉ EXAMPLE

While the WTO and its predecessor, the General Agreement on Tariffs and Trade (GATT), provide examples of how multi-lateral trade arrangements can be constructed, it is important to realize that a CFTA with full participation from Commonwealth states would be one where developed economies are more of a minority. Constructing a CFTA requires an appreciation of linking first and third-world economies – the "North-South" divide.

Within both NAFTA and the EU, nations that would be considered "developing" – Mexico in the former, and some of the previous Soviet bloc states in the latter – are decidedly in the minority. Conventional wisdom dictates that the benefit of such a distribution allows for the economic and social development to occur at a faster pace, as the power of the stronger economies far outstrips the drag that may occur.

In the initial phase, such will be the case with a CFTA. All four charter members are developed economic powers – two being members of the G8 and all four are part of the OECD. The resources to bring one or two poorer states along within the convention would be there, but as the number of new developing nations increases, so, too, does the potential challenge.

For the CFTA to succeed where others have made slow or marginal progress, we must look at attempts at North-South trade – where it succeeded and where it has not. The best example would be the trade agreements signed between the EU and the African, Caribbean and Pacific (ACP) Group of states – the Lomé Conventions.

Concluded in 1975, the Lomé I Convention was designed to allow signatory nations within the developing world access to EU markets in order to "intensify their efforts together for the economic development and social progress of the ACP states." Lomé was created not only to secure trade access for these nations, but to do so "taking account of their respective levels of development, and, in particular, of the need to secure additional benefits for the trade of ACP states." Almost 30 years on, one must ask what the results are. Has Lomé lived up to its expectations? Have the economies of the ACP states been transformed by access to European markets? The answer is that Lomé has had varying degrees of success depending upon where you look.

Lomé has been successful in increasing trade opportunities for ACP states, but it is important to note that this success has been both limited and qualified. By one measure "individual ACP economies performed better in areas where significant preferences were enjoyed compared to those areas where no preferences are enjoyed. While ACP exports to the EU as a whole increased in volume terms between 1988 and 1997 by 3.6%, in those products where the trade preferences provided margins of preference greater than 3%, the expansion in exports in volume terms was 61.9%. This is an export performance that is 17 times better than their general export performance."[67]

Unfortunately, when one looks at all export categories – not just those subscribed by specific trade preference agreements – the numbers are not so encouraging. Indeed "the share of ACP imports into the EU fell from 7% in 1976 to 4% in 2000. Foreign Direct Investments (FDI) from EU to ACP has stagnated. ACP received currently less than 2% of EU foreign direct investment."[68] Moreover:

> *"the exports of other developing countries to the EU grew faster than that of ACP. The exports of ACP countries to the EU grew on average at 2% per annum between 1976 and 2000. The exports from Mediterranean and Latin American countries grew at an average of 6% per annum, while exports from Asian developing countries grew at an average of 12% per annum. Asian countries had replaced ACP as the main developing country exporters to the EU by 1992"*[69]

A main issue must be the state of industrialization in each of the partner states. When talking of allowing ACP states access to the EU, we are really talking about agriculture. Yet this is the one area where the EU, through its

---

[67] Mbuende, Dr. Kaire M., "*ACP-EU Future Trade Relations: Challenges and Opportunities for Eastern and Southern African Countries,*" in Commonwealth Trade Hot Topics, Issue No. 15 (London: Commonwealth Secretariat), p.2
[68] Ibid., p.1
[69] Ibid., p.1

Common Agricultural Policy (CAP) imposes its most stringent barriers. The only nation in Sub-Saharan Africa, for example, that has the level of industrial diversification required to more fully exploit these opportunities is South Africa – not a signatory to the Lomé Conventions.

To protect its own farming sector, the EU is less inclined to encourage imports of competitive products like wheat, and more likely to allow products that do not have available equivalents, such as bananas or citrus fruit. This has the effect of discouraging agricultural diversification in ACP countries and actually making ACP nations more dependent on the EU for those products that are not produced locally in any substantial quantity. Because the EU produces large surpluses as a result of the CAP, and because Europe's production and transportation networks are at such an advanced stage, ACP nations cannot match marginal cost advantages:

> "The Lomé preferences which are geared towards giving Kenyan (among other ACP) exports a price-competitive advantage over other exporters in the EU market are unrealistic. In Kenya, cost disadvantages associated with transport and production inefficiencies run high. Competitors relatively have a superior position in the EU market than Kenyan and other ACP exporters. Similarly, non-price competition is significant in some sectors, for instance competition in quality and promotion, which is relevant for exports of fresh fruit and vegetables."[70]

There is a recurring theme, however, among those ACP states where Lomé has not lived up to its promise. These states share the characteristic traits of instability – political and judicial corruption, abuse of human rights,

---

[70] Otieno-Odek, J., "*Europe and Sub-Saharan Africa Beyond Lome IV Convention*," University of Nairobi, Kenya, http://www.oneworld.org/ecdpm/lome/otieno.htm , 2003 August 26

a lack of freedoms for its citizenry, and a seriously degraded infrastructure for civil society. As Dr. Kaire M. Mbuende concludes "the European Commission believes that there is a need for a new system, as in its view, the past system of non-reciprocal trade preferences extended to ACP countries has on the whole failed to deliver expected results in terms of broader economic and social development. The trade performance of ACP countries have not been impressive."[71]

This was so much the case that the Lomé IV Convention sought to take on the issue of human rights and governance. This, however, does not necessarily guarantee a desired result:

> "The Lomé relationship was incepted during the Cold War. The Convention was then politically neutral. The mid-term review of Lomé IV has abandoned this political neutrality...Article 5 of the revised Lomé IV Convention stipulates that development policy and cooperation shall shall be linked to respect for and enjoyment of fundamental human rights and to the recognition and application of democratic principles, the consolidation of the rule of law and good governance. These principles are stated to constitute an essential element of the Convention. The inclusion of these items in Lomé is laudable. However, the major problem is enforceability."[72]

A large difficulty that arises from conducting such a trading relationship in this manner is that, unfortunately, it feeds into traditional fears and long

---

[71] Mbuende, Dr. Kaire M., "*ACP-EU Future Trade Relations: Challenges and Opportunities for Eastern and Southern African Countries*," in Commonwealth Trade Hot Topics, Issue No. 15, (London: Commonwealth Secretariat), p.1

[72] Otieno-Odek, J., *"Europe and Sub-Saharan Africa Beyond Lome IV Convention,"* University of Nairobi, Kenya, http://www.oneworld.org/ecdpm/lome/otieno.htm , 2003 August 26

held mistrust among developing nations about the motives of the developed world.

> *"It is a common supposition that many developed countries employ the guise of cooperation and partnership arrangements to ensure continuous supply of essential raw materials from developing countries. With this in mind, it is not improbable that even after a genuine design of a good-spirited system of cooperation between developed and developing countries, the former may not make any bona fide efforts to contribute towards meaningful development of the latter; rather, each body seeks ways to outwit the other."*[73]

The very architecture of the Lomé Conventions, it can be said, speaks to an enduring paternalism and the notion that the developing world should be, as what was once said of Canada, "hewers of wood and drawers of water." It grants access to European markets so long as European interests are not affected – however that may be defined. But for what is given, it appears that very little is received in kind. As Paul Sutton observed "the thrust of the Lome Conventions has been conservative. They preserve and permit but they do not of themselves bring either development or prosperity."[74]

International agreements that do not address mutuality fall into such a trap. Negotiating parties are not peers – there is no equal status within the framework and the end result merely perpetuates this imbalance.

The lesson of Lomé is clear – greater trade access, in and of itself, will not bring about a tangible change in the lives of many. Economic freedom is

---

[73] Ibid.
[74] Rosenberg, Mark and Hiskey, Jonathan T., *"Changing Trading Patterns of the Caribbean Basin,"* in Annals, AAPSS, 533, May, 1994, p.105

a product of many interconnected factors, including political freedom, social stability and infrastructure.

As Dr. Kaire M. Mbuende concludes "it is not evident, however, that EPAs [Economic Partnership Agreements] in themselves can provide the necessary stimulus to attract investment in ACP countries. Particularly in the light of poor physical infrastructures, lack of access to inexpensive water and electricity and human resource constraints. This situation is further compounded by the multiplicity of free trade area arrangements, which the EU is concluding with non-ACP states. Why should EU enterprises invest in ACP states to serve EU and ACP markets when they could locate in low wage and high skill zone(s) within an expanding EU?"[75]

So what would help? What, in fact do these nations want and need? As Michael Davenport observes: "many ACPs, while accepting the principle of reciprocity, emphasize flexibility in the process of adjustment to new trading arrangements for small economies, through longer transition periods in the liberalisation process, and also through special safeguard clause(s), freedom from antidumping and other contingent protection, easier rules of origin and technical assistance programmes."[76]

A CFTA, guided from the outset by a basic Charter that combines a minimum code of conduct for member states with a commitment to assist in the orderly development of infrastructure and civil society, may very well succeed in ways that previous attempts at North-South trade have failed.

---

[75] Mbuende, Dr. Kaire M., "*ACP-EU Future Trade Relations: Challenges and Opportunities for Eastern and Southern African Countries*," in Commonwealth Trade Hot Topics, Issue No. 15, (London: Commonwealth Secretariat), p.4
[76] Davenport, Michael, "*ACP-EU negotiations*," in Commonwealth Trade Hot Topics, Issue No. 16, (London: Commonwealth Secretariat, p.4

It can succeed simply because it considers nation-states to be equal entities, and legitimate partners, in the process. The relative size of a given economy, or the affluence of a particular national population would have no bearing on the power exercised within a proposed CFTA. This is important because where nations are treated equitably in such fora, there is a frankness and candor that will yield good policy – good for liberalization and good for development. It will result in a consensus that is more reflective of the realities of individual states, especially those whose economic status is not as advanced as others.

Just as important, it will require the structural reforms in advance of membership, and reserves the right to adjust the pace at which expansion occurs. When applicant states meet the qualifications for joining, and the pace of growth is such that a CFTA is not overwhelmed by the transition process, the organization possesses the ability to move forward.

It is because of the democratic nature of a CFTA structure that one can attempt to avoid the inherent 'paternalism' of a Lomé-type regime. Rather than place members on opposite sides of the table, each state interacts with the whole and arrives at a unified policy. No member state should expect access for a particular good unless that good's trade is deregulated throughout the Association.

Lomé created an environment where ACP states had their role as suppliers of raw materials institutionalized. By default, this also did the same for the EU's role as a supplier of manufactured and value-added products. Ideally, under a CFTA structure, Commonwealth states belonging to the ACP will certainly face competition from developed members with regard to raw material processing, agricultural products, and other primary inputs. Conversely, these developing nations will be able to compete openly on manufacturing, industrial, and other value-added products – something not currently guaranteed by any developed nation, or collection thereof. When coupled with a strategy for development of infrastructure and civil society, the process will be easier to bring to fruition than in current conventional circumstances.

Due to domestic considerations, both in the developed and developing states of a CFTA, agreement could be reached on a schedule for the gradual reduction – and eventual elimination – of tariffs and duties. For developed states, agricultural sectors could find themselves immediately swamped with low-cost products from developing states. On the other hand, developed states could easily flood developing markets with cheaper manufactured goods and high-end products by virtue of access to capital, more efficient production techniques, and economies of scale. Over time, it would be expected that a measured phase-in period would provide economic actors from both ends of the spectrum the time and opportunity to adjust to the realities of functioning in a CFTA.

Despite whatever benefits may have been derived from participation in the Lomé Conventions, the agreement has only served to perpetuate the status quo. In this sense, one can view the creation and expansion of a CFTA as a true paradigm shift that will allow poorer Commonwealth states to achieve meaningful economic progress. A CFTA will demand more, but increased demands should be matched with increased benefits.

## Chapter 7

## COMMONWEALTH TRADE COOPERATION

With the passing of the Sterling Area and the Ottawa Agreements, the formal trade linkages within the Commonwealth have largely disappeared. While leaders have expressed their desire to increase economic cooperation within the organization, effort has largely been placed in building regional trade groupings and in the lobbying effort at the WTO.

Despite this, there have been a number of attempts at advancing the idea of Commonwealth trade, in whole or in part. Not all these initiatives have come to fruition, and for those that have become a reality, the record of achievement has not always been so clear.

Nevertheless, in looking at the following examples, we can learn what has worked, and why. Conversely, we can look to the failed attempts and try to understand what went wrong. It is only through an examination of the successes and failures of Commonwealth trade cooperation that those interested in advancing the notion of a CFTA may be able to craft a better agreement that may avoid repeating the mistakes and miscues of the past.

## UK – Canada Free Trade:

The last real attempt to re-establish a regime of Commonwealth trade liberalization occurred in the fall of 1957, centering around the idea of establishing a Free Trade Zone between Canada and the United Kingdom. What is interesting about this idea is that it did not come from Whitehall.

The proposal was, in many ways, the natural evolution of views held by then Canadian Prime Minister, John Diefenbaker. The ruling Progressive Conservative party had traditionally been more predisposed to closer Empire and Commonwealth ties. Indeed, the party's first leader – and the nation's founding leader – Sir John A. Macdonald, famously stated that "a British subject I was born, a British subject I will die." Under his leadership through the 1870's, Canada pursued what was known as the 'National Policy', a series of economic measures – including high tariffs and duties – designed to develop a domestic industrial and manufacturing base that could withstand competition from the United States.

Much of the motivation for this policy was predicated on curtailing the influence of American industrial interests. These sentiments carried forward as late as 1911 when Liberal Prime Minister Sir Wilfred Laurier was defeated in a general election over his policy of a proposed Reciprocity Treaty with the United States. The popular slogan of Sir Robert Borden's Tories was "No truck or trade with the Yankees."

The economic relationship between Canada and the United States has been traditionally seen by Canadians in a rather ambivalent fashion, with concerns about American economic control waxing and waning – usually within the context of larger political trends. Despite the ebb and flow of sentiment, two contradictory trends have developed. While political sentiments about perceived American domination of Canadian economic interests have remained fairly strong, so too has the level of American activity in the Canadian economy.

It was in this environment that Diefenbaker sought a policy that would provide a counterbalance to American influence in Canada. As leader of a party that was traditionally supportive of the Empire and Commonwealth, it was natural that he saw this counterbalance in the guise of the United Kingdom.

Starting in 1957, Diefenbaker began to express to members of his cabinet a desire to shift a significant portion of Canadian imports away from US suppliers toward sources from the UK. At this time, he had indicated that the goal should be to 'substitute' sources for up to 15 percent of Canada's total imports of goods and services. It was also clear that this process was to lay the groundwork for a larger Commonwealth-wide project in the future.

The beginning of this process occurred on July 3, 1957 during a meeting of Commonwealth Prime Ministers in London. During the meeting, Prime Minister Diefenbaker outlined the challenge he saw for the Canadian economy and its future prospects, that "she had in fact received considerable investment from the USA which now far outstripped the UK as the chief foreign investor in Canada and was in a position to dominate the basic industries such as oil, copper, etc…"[77]

Diefenbaker stated that "within the foreseeable future the USA demand for many of these materials would outstrip the domestic reserves and it was for this reason that American interests have been extending their interests in our industries to an extent which might challenge Canada's economic freedom."[78] He went on to discuss a practice whereby American companies would establish Canadian subsidiaries, but refuse any Canadian participation, either as shareholders, or in having "any say in its development."[79]

It was in this light that an invitation was extended to attend a Commonwealth trade and economic conference. From the beginning, however, various leaders expressed different positions.

The British government made clear their focus on joining the newly proposed European Free Trade Area (EFTA), "as otherwise Germany might eventually dominate Europe from the economic point of view and displace Britain from many of her foreign markets."[80]

Sir Robert Menzies, Prime Minister of Australia, had initially been supportive of the idea of a conference, but "a few days later he appeared to have completely changed his mind."[81] His concern focused on the desire not to reproduce the Ottawa Agreements of 1932, feeling that "Australia's

---

[77] Canada, Dept. of External Affairs, External Affairs, Vol. 24 – 343, *Chapter III, Commonwealth Relations, Part 2, Minutes of Meeting*, Ottawa, July 3, 1957
[78] Ibid., July 3, 1957
[79] Ibid., July 3, 1957
[80] Ibid., July 3, 1957
[81] Ibid., July 3, 1957

freedom of movement was restricted"[82] by them. Menzies countered that the answer to raising living standards in southwest Asia was in "expanding trade with a revitalized Japan."[83] Thomas L. Macdonald, New Zealand's External Affairs Minister, also concurred with this view.

In the end, Prime Minister Macmillan lent his support to the Canadian initiative, adding that his government "would not have the position of Commonwealth agricultural products in the UK market interfered with by the European Free Trade Area scheme."[84]

Following up on the discussions at the Commonwealth leaders' summit, a meeting of Canadian officials, including the Ministers of Finance and Trade, as well as the Canadian Ambassador to the United States, took place on July 11, 1957. The discussion centred around the tone of the planned conference. From Canada's standpoint, the message to be put forth was that "the U.S. was a good neighbour and antipathy towards her was not the reason for prompting the government to seek a wider diversification of markets. What was sought was a strengthening of Commonwealth ties through an increase in Commonwealth trade."[85]

In anticipation of a visit from Prime Minister Menzies within the month, emphasis was placed on preparing for those meetings. The sense was that Australia was prepared to give up preferences in her trade with the UK if it meant more trade elsewhere – particularly in Europe and Japan. Moreover, it was felt "Australia had not had much trade with Canada which would make

---

[82] Ibid., July 3, 1957
[83] Ibid., July 3, 1957
[84] Ibid., July 3, 1957
[85] Canada, Dept. of External Affairs, *External Affairs*, Vol. 24-343, *Chapter III, Commonwealth Relations, Part 2, Minutes of Meeting*, Ottawa, July 11, 1957.

the discussions with Mr. Menzies not too easy."[86] The Canadian approach, therefore, was to be that "the important thing was to maintain Commonwealth trade."[87]

In the broader sense, it was agreed that the collective approach in pursuing a Commonwealth trade agreement was needed. According to the officials:

> *"Given the existing framework of current conditions, which included the fact that no new preferences could be expected, the need for capital particularly by the under-developed members, etc., it seemed that any proposed Commonwealth discussions would lead into consideration of the dollar-sterling area position and the prospects of sterling convertibility."*[88]

Despite the clear challenges to brokering any sort of deal, in a series of meetings and communications between British and Canadian government officials from August to October of that year, the details of a Canada-UK Free Trade Agreement were discussed. These private talks were running concurrently with preparations for a Commonwealth Trade and Economic summit to be held at Mont Tremblant, Quebec in late September. From the beginning, however, both sides were somewhat hampered by issues that would either place into jeopardy relations with other nations, or would create economic conditions that were below expectations, or clearly disadvantageous.

---

[86] Ibid., July 11, 1957.
[87] Ibid., July 11, 1957.
[88] Ibid., July 11, 1957.

The first challenge was the 15 percent target. While Prime Minister Diefenbaker set the goal and was committed to it, members of his cabinet, including the Finance Minister, the Minister of Trade, and senior bureaucrats were skeptical that it could be easily attained.

On August 12, 1957, R.B. Bryce, the Secretary to the Cabinet, sent a memo to Diefenbaker that included a detailed study by the Finance Department on the feasibility of such a plan. Bryce wrote that there were "many serious difficulties" with its implementation and that "to divert as much as 15% in the way considered would require quite drastic action."[89]

Finance Department officials estimated that diverting 15 per cent of Canadian imports from the US to Britain would require the UK's share of imports increasing from 8.5 per cent (in 1956) to 19.5 per cent.[90] In dollar terms, it would require Canadian imports of British goods to rise from $485 million to about $1.11 billion – an increase of 130 per cent.[91] This seemed all the more daunting when they had concluded "about 56 per cent of the Canadian import market offers little opportunity for trade diversion from the United States to the United Kingdom."[92] Indeed, Britain's share of Canadian imports had only reached the target level in only five years between 1914 and 1957.[93]

It was noted, however, that this exception to the overall declining trend was between 1932 and 1936, when Britain's average share of Canadian imports rose by roughly 5 per cent over levels in 1930-31, and that "the

---

[89] Ibid., July 11, 1957.
[90] Ibid., July 11, 1957.
[91] Ibid., July 11, 1957.
[92] Ibid., July 11, 1957.
[93] Ibid., July 11, 1957.

improvement in Britain's position at that time can be ascribed to the substantially wider preferential margins granted by the 1932 Empire Agreements."[94]

Moreover, to achieve this target, it would be necessary to take drastic action, namely open government interventions against goods imported from the United States. It was not enough to make British goods cheaper – American goods had to become more expensive. This means imposing tariff restrictions that, in the view of the officials, would invite a hostile reaction from Washington, and a breach of Canada's obligations under the GATT. British officials were supportive of the target, in theory, but also shared Canadian concerns about a potential US reaction, noting that the existing trade agreements between the United States and the UK were up for renewal within the year.

What made this particular discussion about diversion of US trade all the more interesting was that it occurred only five days after the Associated Press had reported that while on a visit to Rio de Janeiro, a member of the Eisenhower administration called for a hemispheric common market. Eric Johnston, the chairman of the President's international economic advisory board, made his comments in a speech before the American Chamber of Commerce of Brazil.

This, however, was a slight distraction. Aware of protectionist sentiments in Congress, the official reaction from the White House was that Mr. Johnston "expresses his own views and that no government policy has yet

---

[94] Ibid., July 11, 1957.

been formulated or is being discussed about a common market in the Western Hemisphere."[95]

From the beginning, the UK was reluctant to expand the scope of the talks beyond the two principals. The British position was that, with the exception of Australia and New Zealand, other Commonwealth states had not developed enough economically to be good and reliable partners in such an enterprise; that is, that none of those states had developed a large enough consumer class to make a larger project viable. Moreover, it was feared that these states would counter an invitation with demands for financial aid from both the UK and Canada – something that neither country wished to entertain outside existing commitments through the Colombo Plan.

Another issue was the dual focus of UK trade policy that, in many ways, set itself up with competing goals. While Britain was still interested in developing Commonwealth trade through the long term, it also had great interest in developing closer ties to Europe, either through the European Free Trade Area (EFTA), or the still-nascent European Economic Community (EEC). Indeed, the UK had enunciated a strategy of being committed to both groups in a trade relationship, hoping to act as a 'bridge' between her former colonies and the rest of Europe.

The problem with the strategy went beyond the normal distractions of maintaining a dual focus. Commonwealth members such as Canada and Australia wanted greater guarantees of access to Europe than what a British 'intermediary' would offer. Indeed, Canada also enquired about the possibility of joining a European trade grouping itself. On the other side, European states were wary of Britain's reluctance to commit wholly to the

---

[95] "*Seek Common Market for this Hemisphere*," The Globe and Mail, Toronto, August 8, 1957.

European project. French President Charles de Gaulle was pre-eminent among those who voiced concerns with the UK policy.

Beyond the larger questions of international trade relations, there were real concerns as to whether the relationship would yield tangible benefits to both parties. According to Canadian finance department officials, it was felt that while the UK would benefit greatly by this access, some Canadian industries, particularly textiles manufacturing, would be decimated. Moreover, it was felt that the import substitution would be mostly confined to consumer non-durables, such as small appliances, liquor products, and such.

Despite the indication that a Free Trade Area, as negotiated under these terms, would not be an equitable proposition, the Canadian government was still interested in creating a counterweight to American economic influence. Prime Minister Diefenbaker had gone so far as to make clear that he would support a deal even if the accrued benefits were 60/40 in favour of the UK. Unfortunately, in the eyes of those representing Canada in these talks, even this target did not seem attainable.

Beyond this lay the question of how the broader economic relationship within the Commonwealth was to be constructed. It was clear that the position of the Diefenbaker government was to use an initial Canada-UK agreement as a starting point for a larger Commonwealth-wide effort. In this strategy, one would have envisioned the addition of other members to the agreement, much as what has happened in the present with Mexico's entry into NAFTA, and the addition of states into the European Union. The British position, to the contrary, was to conclude a specifically bilateral arrangement. When pressed, however, the UK negotiating team did concede that if Australia or New Zealand were to press for a similar agreement, they would entertain the idea seriously.

Rather than pursue a multilateral framework, the Macmillan government's strategy was that of creating a network of bilateral arrangements with individual Commonwealth states. This, of course, gave the appearance of wanting to resurrect the old Empire trading regime, where Britain acted as the hub for a larger Commonwealth system. Commonwealth countries would, in essence, need to use Britain as an intermediary, rather than be able to develop relationships between one another.

Eventually, in the run up to the Mont Tremblant conference, some aspects of the talks were leaked to the press. While neither the Canadian or the UK governments denied that they were exploring a possible free trade deal, one of the UK diplomats participating in the negotiations, Sir Selwyn Lloyd, stated that the idea was essentially a Canadian proposition, and that the Macmillan government felt somewhat obligated to explore a relationship with one of her former dominions.[96] In addition, the UK negotiating team had requested that approval of a deal be expedited. Canadian officials judged this stance as being politically motivated, possibly as a means of gaining leverage in dealing with European states, or with Washington.

In the end, the idea was laid to rest by mutual consent. From this point forward, Britain focused her attention on trade ties to Europe, while Canada reconciled with the trend of ever increasing integration into a North American economy. As George Grant wrote in his "Lament for a Nation":

---

[96] Canada, Department of External Affairs, External Affairs, Vol. 24 – 343, *Chapter III, Commonwealth Relations, Part 2, Minutes of Meeting*, Ottawa, July 11, 1957

"*The pattern of Canadian trade could not be changed in the way Diefenbaker suggested in 1957. He understood this himself by the time he turned down the United Kingdom's later proposals for a free-trade area with Canada. After such a refusal, the English could not stomach the appeal he made for the Commonwealth in London...It seemed the stuff of fantasy, not a viable alternative.*"[97]

In retrospect, one could see the idea of a Canada-UK Free Trade Agreement as being flawed from the beginning. First, there was no clear rationale for the idea, save for a reaction to American economic power. Secondly, it is not clear that either side was entering into an agreement for reasons that were compatible, or that the relationship would give both parties an approximate benefit. Also, while it is not clear whether Canada was negotiating as a means of moving a bilateral agenda with the US, it is equally uncertain as to whether the UK was not using the issue as a means of moving its trade agenda with Europe – especially in dealing with lukewarm acceptance from France. Finally, the reluctance to broaden the scope of an agreement to include other Commonwealth partners simply perpetuated the policy of having Britain act as the centrepoint of Commonwealth economic activity, rather than a more diffuse and broad-based structure – a traditional sticking point with the more developed dominions.

So what has changed with respect to today? First, both Canada and the UK have developed enough economically so as to compliment each other's attributes. Also, in the post-Cold war world, solidarity with the US on economic matters exists only in the context of WTO obligations, to which virtually every nation on earth has committed itself. In addition, in today's globalized economy, and with many issues of governance and development

---

[97] George Grant, *"Lament for a Nation,"* (Montreal: McGill-Queen's University Press), 1965, p. 51

on the table, attitudes within and outside the national loci of power are more appreciative of such a concept. Most importantly, there has been a maturing of opinions and attitudes within the Commonwealth. The UK has long dispensed with the pretenses of Empire, while other Commonwealth members are, both physically and psychologically, equal to Britain in the community of nations. This may very well be the most important factor in allowing ourselves to consider the possibility of Commonwealth free trade.

<u>CARICOM</u>

While many Commonwealth nations have negotiated bilateral trade agreements with one another, none have attempted to bring together so many parties to so high a level of integration as the Caribbean Community and Common Market, or CARICOM. Although the scale of coordination and economic integration may be modest when compared to NAFTA or the EU it, nonetheless, provides some insights into the opportunities and challenges that would face the founders of a CFTA. Moreover, as the majority of CARICOM member states are also Commonwealth nations, their participation in a CFTA is possible, if not probable.

In this respect, it is useful to look at both the history of CARICOM and the practical elements of Caribbean trade, both internally and beyond the region.

The creation of CARICOM was the result of an effort to push for greater regional integration, first initiated with the British West Indies (BWI) Federation in 1958. The BWI Federation plan was to be a federal style government drawn from 10 member islands. Although a plan for a Customs Union was drawn up, economic aspects of the Federation were not made a priority in the beginning.

Economically, the region remained as it had been, with no attempt at trade liberalization between member countries. The Federation came to an end in 1962, but this experiment did place greater regional cooperation in the Caribbean on the agenda. It meant the beginning of more serious efforts to strengthen ties.

In 1962, the Government of Trinidad and Tobago proposed the creation of a Caribbean Community, consisting not only of the 10 members of the Federation, but also of the three Guianas and all the islands of the Caribbean Sea - both independent and non-independent.

The first Heads of Government Conference was convened in Trinidad and Tobago in July 1963. This Conference was attended by the leaders of Barbados, British Guiana, Jamaica, and Trinidad and Tobago. At this Conference, the leaders of the four Caribbean Countries all spoke clearly of the need for close cooperation with Europe, Africa and Latin America.

The first Heads of Government Conference proved to be the first in a series of Conferences among the leaders of Commonwealth Caribbean Countries. In 1965, talks between the Premiers of Barbados and British Guiana and the Chief Minister of Antigua on the possible establishment of a Free Trade Area led to the signing of an agreement at Dickenson Bay, Antigua, to set up the Caribbean Free Trade Association (CARIFTA).

To ensure the widest possible degree of cooperation among all the Commonwealth Caribbean territories, the actual start of the Association was delayed in order to allow the rest of the Region, Trinidad and Tobago and Jamaica and all the Windward and Leeward islands to become members.

It was agreed that the Free Trade Association was to be the beginning of what would eventually become a Caribbean Common Market.

In recognition of their special development challenges, several special provisions were agreed upon for the benefit of the seven Member States that now make up the Organization of Eastern Caribbean States (OECS) and Belize.

CARIFTA came into effect on May 1, 1968, with the participation of Antigua, Barbados, Trinidad and Tobago and Guyana. Dominica, Grenada, St. Kitts, Nevis, Anguilla, St. Lucia and St. Vincent entered in July, with Jamaica and Montserrat joining on August 1, 1968. British Honduras (Belize) became a member in 1971. Following CARIFTA was the establishment of the Commonwealth Caribbean Regional Secretariat in 1968, and the Caribbean Development Bank (CDB) in 1969.

In October 1972, Caribbean Leaders decided to transform CARIFTA into a Common Market and establish the Caribbean Community. The Accord to establish the Community was signed the following year by all CARIFTA states, except Antigua and Montserrat.

The Caribbean Community and Common Market (CARICOM) was established by the Treaty of Chaguaramas on August 1, 1973. The Bahamas became the 13th member of the Community on July 4, 1983, but not a member of the Common Market. In 1991, the British Virgin Islands, and the Turks and Caicos became Associate Members of CARICOM, followed by Anguilla in 1999, the Cayman Islands in 2002, and Bermuda in 2003.

A number of states in Latin America and the wider Caribbean enjoy Observer status within the Community. Puerto Rico, a Territory of the USA, is also seeking closer ties with CARICOM.

Suriname became the 14th Member State of the Caribbean Community on July 4, 1995.

Haiti became the first French-speaking Caribbean State to become a full member of CARICOM in 2002. The CARICOM Secretariat established an office in the capital, Port-au-Prince, to provide technical assistance to the Government.

From its inception, the CARICOM has concentrated on the promotion of functional cooperation, especially in relation to human and social development, and in integrating the economies of member states. The independent Member States however, have also been pursuing a coordinated foreign policy. Other areas of coordination include: external trade negotiations, air transport and maritime infrastructure policy and development; telecommunications policy; and employment generation.

At the CARICOM Heads of Government Meeting in 1987, the Prime Minister of Barbados, Erskine Sandiford, advanced the concept of a representative institution that would associate the people of the Region, through their chosen representatives. Two years later, Barbados followed up with a discussion paper outlining the proposal to the Conference.

In March 1990, agreement was reached on the establishment of the proposed body, the Assembly of Caribbean Community Parliamentarians (ACCP). The inaugural sitting of the Assembly took place in Barbados on

May 27-29, 1996. There have been two other sittings since - in Grenada in 1999 and Belize in 2000.

Since this time, CARICOM have discussed governance and human rights issues, including the establishment of a Caribbean Court of Justice, and the adoption of civil society standards.

CARICOM has had some degree of success in achieving greater economic integration among its members. For example, in 1996, 72% of all of Barbados' intraregional imports and 84.5% of Jamaica's came from Trinidad and Tobago. In 1995 member states agreed to the free movement of CARICOM Nationals who were university graduates. Eleven member states have already completed the legislative process to enact this decision.[98]

Despite this positive movement, there has been a great deal of criticism of CARICOM's attempts at brining economic integration to a substantial level. This is due mainly because of the sense that agreements made between the Heads of Governments and Ministerial Councils remain in paper form, that CARICOM members lack the political will to enforce them. It is also argued that because CARICOM lacks this ability, there is no power to sanction member states that fail to comply with agreements made. In fact this was the concern aired by President Arthur N. R. Robinson in the Time for Action Report of the West Indian Commission, 1992.[99]

The Common External Tariff, a key element of any customs union, has not been adopted by all member states. Also, there are still member states that have failed to remove existing import duties and other trade barriers for

---

[98] Trinidad and Tobago Chamber of Industry and Commerce - *Caricom countries need to keep to their agreements*, February 07, 2002, http://www.chamber.org.tt/article_archive/column/070202.htm
[99] Ibid.

trade intra regionally. Critics have further charged that the gains through the freeing of trade have been limited since there has not been an overall increase in the share of the regional market being captured by CARICOM compared to the rest of the world.[100]

Some would argue that the greater challenge lies not within the membership of CARICOM, but in the "implementation of free trade arrangements and the changing political alliances throughout the global community"[101]

The primary means by which the Caribbean regions trades beyond is through its agreements with the United States (Caribbean Basin Initiative) and the European Union (the Lomé and Cotonou Agreements). Both agreements give Caribbean states preferences in traditional (agricultural) and nontraditional (manufacturing) products. The impact that each has had, however, has been decidedly different. "Whereas the CBI has stimulated nontraditional exports – namely, apparel – while retaining restrictions on traditional agricultural products, the Lome and its associated protocols have provided a guaranteed market for Caribbean agricultural exports while discouraging nontraditional products."[102]

With reference to the Caribbean Basin Initiative (CBI) the benefit to the region has been less than stellar. "As the value of US imports increased 50 percent between 1984 and 1990, CBI country exports to the United States declined 13 percent despite the addition, in 1990, of Nicaragua to the

---

[100] Ibid.
[101] Mark Rosenberg and Jonathan T. Hiskey, *"Changing Trading Patterns of the Caribbean Basin,"* in Annals, AAPSS, 533, May, 1994, p,100
[102] Mark Rosenberg and Jonathan T. Hiskey, *"Changing Trading Patterns of the Caribbean Basin,"* p.101

program."[103] Also, while the bright spot of CBI trade has been its textiles and apparel exports, Mexico's entry into NAFTA gives it a clear advantage over Caribbean states in exporting these products into the United States. With more progressive foreign investment rules, its large domestic market, as well as its proximity to the US, membership in NAFTA gives Mexico a clear and qualitative advantage over their Caribbean competitors.[104]

In addition to this situation is the commitment of Washington to continuing the CBI. Myles Frechette, the former US Trade Representative for Latin America, the Caribbean, and Africa, offered a cautionary note, adding that in 1990 the Clinton administration had a great challenge in getting Congress to approve the CBI a permanent program.[105] Frechette went further in adding "the West Indian Commission's call for CARICOM to obtain from the NAFTA parties the same access achieved by Mexico without providing reciprocal concessions strikes us as unrealistic."[106]

The other main mode of access for CARICOM trade is through the Lomé (now Cotonou) agreements. While it would appear that this trade regime constitutes a formal and solid policy between two parties. In practice, this could not be further from the truth. Trade occurs on two tracks – as an arrangement between the EU and the Caribbean region, and as a series of bilateral agreements between particular Caribbean states and their former colonial powers.

---

[103] Mark Rosenberg and Jonathan T. Hiskey, *"Changing Trading Patterns of the Caribbean Basin,"* in Annals, AAPSS, 533, May, 1994, p,101
[104] Ibid., p,102
[105] Ibid., p,103
[106] Ibid.,, p,103

These two tracks, rather than compliment each other, serve only to undermine their stated goals. According to Paul Sutton "it is a misnomer to talk of 'European' policy to the Caribbean. There has to date been no one fully articulated European policy but rather a cluster of separate foreign policies focused on distinctive parts of the region."[107] The lack of policy coherence in European-Caribbean trade has had a deleterious effect on greater economic integration in the region as well:

> *"Among the CARICOM nations, there exists a widening split between countries still tied predominantly to their former colonial powers and those that have succeeded in establishing a presence in the North American market. This division will be exacerbated with the contrast between the US emphasis on reciprocity and Europe's focus on preferential access."*[108]

From the implementation of the first Lome Convention in 1975, to the expiry of the fourth in 2000, Caribbean states – along with other states in Africa and the Pacific – were granted preferential market access to the EU. It is fair to say, however, that the continuance of this regime is not assured. Pressure from the WTO, the United States, and emerging players such as China are, in themselves, difficult for Brussels to ignore. Even if the EU were able to resist and officially remain determined to sustain these relationships, one must consider the impact of the recent EU expansion into eastern Europe, and the possibility of an offer of membership to Turkey in the future. Internal political and economic matters always determine external policies. Where the interests of domestic constituencies differ from those of foreign actors, nations – and supra-national entities – will always choose in their own self-interest. CARICOM interests, when they are at variance with

---

[107] Ibid., p,105
[108] Ibid., p,105

domestic interests within the EU or NAFTA, will be placed at a clear disadvantage. Without the ability to mount a powerful lobby, or introduce other bilateral and multilateral issues as leverage, it is hard to see how this trend may be reversed.

It is evident that the success of CARICOM economies depends upon dependable market access to the developed world, the opportunity for economic diversification, access to capital and investment, and to become part of a larger dialogue that will allow individuals to maintain democratic controls and set community standards based on a clear set of predetermined rules. It is in this respect that one can see a natural affinity for what a Commonwealth Free Trade Association represents.

## *NEPAD*

Though not exclusively a Commonwealth based initiative, the New Partnership for Africa's Development (NEPAD) warrants mention for two particular reasons. First, Commonwealth members, notably South Africa, figure prominently in the organization's inception, as well as in its functioning. Secondly, the guiding principles of NEPAD are a natural compliment to what a CFTA would call upon for qualification to join its ranks.

NEPAD was developed in 2001, largely through the efforts of two African leaders, Presidents Thabo Mbeki of South Africa and Abdoulaye Wade of Senegal. Recognizing the challenges facing the continent, and fully aware of other initiatives that have failed to deliver tangible results, NEPAD has been purposefully designed to approach issues from a different perspective.

First, unlike its predecessors, NEPAD is an African initiative – run for Africans by Africans. In this respect, it is able to garner more political legitimacy than other shared programs that give the sense that decisions are being made elsewhere. In addition, NEPAD is less focused on securing outside resources, and more intent on helping African states undertake the political and economic reforms necessary to garner the respect and support of the international community.

The NEPAD agreement calls for African leaders to work collectively for the following goals, including "promoting and protecting democracy and human rights...by developing clear standards of accountability, transparency and participatory governance; restoring and maintaining macroeconomic stability...and introducing appropriate institutional frameworks; instituting transparent legal and regulatory frameworks for financial markets and the auditing of private companies and the public sector; and revitalizing and extending the provision of education, technical training and health services..."[109]

In setting out this ambitious agenda, the agreement explains "our peoples, in spite of the present difficulties, must regain confidence in their genius and their capacity to face obstacles and be involved in the building of the new Africa."[110] It goes on to say that NEPAD is "an expression of the

---

[109] The New Partnership for Africa's Development (NEPAD) Agreement, October 2001, http://www.uneca.org/eca_resources/Conference_Reports_and_Other_Documents/nepad/NEPAD.htm, , p.10.
[110] Ibid., p.12

commitment of Africa's leaders to translate the deep popular will into action."[111]

The hope for NEPAD is to "develop the capacity to sustain growth levels required to achieve poverty reduction and sustainable development."[112] This goal, of course, is easier said than done. Those who helped develop this initiative, and have seen an organizational structure take root, are aware that the key to success "depends on other factors such as infrastructure, capital accumulation, human capital, institutions, structural diversification, competitiveness, health, and good stewardship of the environment."[113]

So how does this agenda translate into a set plan of defined goals? NEPAD, itself, has interpreted the elements of a successful strategy. It has, for example, set the following targets to be attained by 2015:

- achieving and sustaining a GDP growth rate exceeding 7 per cent, annualized;

- cutting the number of people living in extreme poverty in half;

- having all school age children enrolled in primary schools;

- eliminating systemic barriers to women in education (by 2005);

- reducing infant and child mortality rates by 66 per cent;

---
[111] Ibid., p.12
[112] Ibid., p.13
[113] Ibid., p.13

- reducing maternal mortality rates by 75 per cent;

- providing full access for reproductive health services; and,

- implementing national strategies for sustainable development.[114]

The centrepiece of NEPAD's action on compliance is what is called the African Peer Review Mechanism, or APRM. Administered through the African Union (AU), the APRM was created to help African states meet their "obligations on political, corporate and economic governance and conflict resolution."[115] Again, although African leaders have consulted closely with organizations such as the OECD and the European Union on this issue, it is still a 'Made in Africa' initiative.

The APRM is a volunteer compact. The preconditions are to sign the NEPAD Declaration on Democracy, Political, Economic and Corporate Governance, and to agree to periodic peer reviews to assess compliance. The base review is done 18 months after ratification of the agreement. Followups are done within three to five years thereafter, with the possibility of *ad hoc* reviews where special circumstances warrant.

The review process consists of five stages, beginning with background research. Subsequent to this, NEPAD representatives conduct field consultations to assess performance on key governance and development issues. Beyond this, the review process follows two tracks – economic and political. Because NEPAD's mandate is to facilitate sustainable economic

---

[114] Ibid., p.14

[115] Tom Nevin, "*Nepad – what is it and what can it really do?*", African Business, April, 2003, p. 31

growth, the peer review reports are largely confined to matters of political, economic and corporate governance.

Follow up reviews are conducted by what is referred to as a 'Panel of Eminent Persons.' Supported with technical expertise from various pan-African institutions, a panel of five to seven prominent persons would lead the review. The benchmarks for this review were drafted in November of 2003, in time for the various participants to ratify the APRM.

The initial funding for this initiative comes from a combination of assessed contributions from member states (based on GDP), and contributions from donor countries, development agencies and unconditional grants from international organizations. The question of foreign influence has been raised in this respect, and because of the desire to make NEPAD a full function of the African Union, future funding for the APRM will come from the AU membership as a regular budgetary allocation.

Nevertheless, NEPAD is not immune from criticism from those who see its progress as too slow, or its objectives as too timid:

> "Its impotency on Zimbabwe, its emasculated peer review programme and its helplessness in other African crises all point to good intentions going nowhere and costing a lot of money. The international financial community has been quick to shower Nepad with diplomatic bouquets, but reluctant to come up with any meaningful funding."[116]

---

[116] Nevin, Tom, "*Nepad – what is it and what can it really do?*", African Business, April, 2003, p. 30

As Jakkie Cilliers observed "it is equally evident that the NEPAD partners and the donor community, the G8 in particular, have been guilty of creating expectations around the Partnership and its peer review mechanism that were practically unrealistic and politically impossible."[117]

Also, there may be issues of representation and a truly shared commitment beyond words. At this point, for example, "virtually all Nepad's infrastructure is based in South Africa and, of growing concern to South African taxpayers, being funded almost exclusively by that country."[118]

After three years, is it too early to ask whether NEPAD is making a difference? Is it too soon to gauge the effectiveness of the partnership in making some progress? Such an examination does not lend itself to easy answers. One may be quick to point out that the situation in Zimbabwe has actually deteriorated further over this time. To be fair, however, one must also consider the continued stability in South Africa, as well as the improved conditions in Uganda, Nigeria and Kenya. While it would be difficult to attribute these cases, good and bad, to the involvement of NEPAD, if it has had any impact, then the balance sheet seems to be tipped in its favour. Given that the APRM did not come into effect until 2003, one could argue that NEPAD has earned neither brickbats nor bouquets as of yet.

This, however, is not a criticism of NEPAD, but merely recognition of the challenges that yet remain. Cilliers cautions that the consensual approach described as "peer learning" may face a challenge because "there is…no requirement for countries that accede to NEPAD and the APRM to meet

---

[117] Cilliers, Jakkie, "*NEPAD's Peer Review Mechanism*", Institute for Security Studies Occasional Paper No. 64 – November 2002., p.12
[118] Nevin, Tom, "*Nepad – what is it and what can it really do?*", African Business, April, 2003, p.30

predetermined standards"[119] and that "the accession by countries such as Zimbabwe and Libya under their present leadership does not present NEPAD with an immediate problem – but will inevitably do so in due course if these countries do not change their style of government significantly."[120] The inherent danger, of course, is a process guided not by measurable benchmarks and set standards, but an ephemeral definition of "best practices" that is merely a politically expedient lowest common denominator.

Beyond that, we must concede that NEPAD is still a step in the right direction. Any solution to the problems of a particular region needs to be homegrown. Without the necessary level of commitment, or 'buy-in,' no solution will succeed. Also, reducing poverty, crime and corruption – while reinforcing civil society – is an indispensable precondition for economic and social development. It may be partly contrived to give the developed world what it wants, but it certainly is designed to give the peoples of Africa what they need.

As Dave Malcolmson, NEPAD's International Liaison Manager, points out "for peer review to succeed, it must be non-confrontational and provide peer learning and peer pressure. It should not be used as a sanctioning mechanism, and should be considered voluntary."[121]

In essence, what we can see with NEPAD is a genuine recognition among African leaders that no solution to their economic and social problems will come without the peoples of Africa taking ownership of their

---

[119] Cilliers, Jakkie, "*NEPAD's Peer Review Mechanism*", Institute for Security Studies Occasional Paper No. 64 – November 2002, p.13
[120] Cilliers, Jakkie, "*NEPAD's Peer Review Mechanism*", p.13
[121] Nevin, Tom, "*Nepad – what is it and what can it really do?*", African Business, April, 2003, p. 31

destiny. A transformation of the continent can only be achieved when Africa and the developed world commit themselves to their particular duties – one to transform their nations into modern and representative democracies with a vibrant civil society; the other to fully accept these peoples into the global economy without reservation.

A CFTA would present a clear commitment by both sides to the spirit of NEPAD. Commonwealth nations in Africa who have already embraced NEPAD need only keep those promises, and in return, nations such as Australia, Canada, and the United Kingdom would grant them the access to trade and capital they need to develop and nurture their economy, and to finance the institutions that are recognized as the hallmarks of a modern democracy and civil society.

As NEPAD's Commonwealth members undergo this transformation, one can argue that the African Union's broader goals become much easier to attain, for among themselves, they will be able to see a positive example of North-South cooperation, and will have, on their own continent, nations capable of taking a leadership role within a new Africa.

## *Australia-New Zealand Closer Economic Relations Trade Agreement (ANZCERTA)*

For those seeking a possible template for economic cooperation between developed Commonwealth nations, the Australia – New Zealand Closer Economic Relations Trade Agreement (ANZCERTA) provides a positive and workable example of what can be achieved.

ANZCERTA is the culmination of a process that began in 1966, with the original Australia New Zealand Free Trade Agreement. This relationship had, by the latter part of the 1970's, brought about "the removal of tariffs and quantitative restrictions on 80 per cent of trans-Tasman trade."[122]

The desire to move beyond the existing FTA was not due to any failure of the process. In fact, it had become clear that it had been very successful within its remit, and that if the two parties were interested in moving even further in the direction of trade liberalization, a new agreement would be required. Of special interest to Australia, for example, was a mechanism for removing the import licensing restrictions in place in New Zealand.[123]

Beginning in 1980, both countries began the process of negotiating "closer economic relations" in order to "forward the proposition that an appropriately structured closer economic relationship would benefit the international competitiveness of both countries and improve living standards" that would "not conflict with an outward-looking approach to trade; nor should it interfere with each country's obligations under the GATT and other multilateral and bilateral trade agreements."[124]

ANZCERTA was ratified and came into effect in 1983, with the proviso that it would undergo comprehensive reviews in 1988 and 1992 to assess its progress at that point. It was through this review process that additional protocols were introduced, including agreements on technical barriers to trade, government purchasing, industry assistance, business-law harmonization, export restrictions and the harmonization of customs rules.

---

[122] "*Closer Economic Relations – A Background Guide to the Australia-New Zealand Economic Relationship*", Department of Foreign Affairs and Trade, Commonwealth of Australia, February 1997, p.6
[123] Ibid., p.7
[124] Ibid., p.7

Further innovations focused on advancing trade and investment, including mutual recognition, harmonizing standards, and efforts to work toward a harmonization of business law between the two countries.

There are, of course, notable exceptions within the Agreement that either party can exercise, with the proviso that they are not used "as a means of arbitrary or unjustified discrimination or as a disguised restriction on trade."[125] Among the allowable justifications are measures that protect "essential security interests", public morals and the prevention of criminal activity; health and human, animal or plant life; intellectual or industrial property rights; the ability to prevent unfair or deceptive practices; and the application of regulatory standards for classifying and grading goods.

As much as ANZCERTA has enabled closer economic cooperation between Australia and New Zealand, it is, by no means, an inward looking relationship. In recent years, relationships have been initiated with the nations of the ASEAN Free Trade Area (AFTA) and those of the South American trading group MERCOSUR.

At the heart of trans-Tasman trade policy is a recognition that both Australia and New Zealand, despite the success of their relationship, still needs to find its place in a broader world trading system. As John Kunkel states about Australia's position in this matter, her "trading interests are thus broadly-based and geographically diverse. But without a natural home in a trading bloc, its room to maneuver may not always be what it is today."[126] This reality "underpins Australia's support for the multilateral system and a

---

[125] Ibid., p.9
[126] Kunkel, John, "*Australian trade policy in an age of globalisation,*" Australian Journal of International Affairs, Vol. 56, No. 2, 2002, p.240

strong WTO that seeks to enforce the rule of law on larger powers like the United States, the European Union (EU) and Japan."[127]

The challenge for Australia and New Zealand comes from an international trading regime that is increasingly "...is cluttered with new demands for global governance, an increasingly assertive bloc of poor countries, proliferating regional and bilateral trade agreements, and calls to 'democratise' trade."[128] For each of these countries, success will depend upon how each "...is to deploy its limited resources and clout where they can best serve the national interest."[129]

It is evident by reviewing the long history of trans-Tasman trade, as well as the scope of the agreements negotiated, that the relationship has been positive and beneficial for both nations. Speaking on the 20th anniversary of the Agreement, Australia's Trade Minister, the Hon. Mark Vaile, commented that "the Australia-New Zealand CER agreement is the most comprehensive, effective and mutually compatible free trade agreement in the world and one of the most successful examples of economic integration."[130] According to Vaile "the CER has created substantial jobs and wealth in both countries. Two-way trade with New Zealand has expanded 500 per cent since CER was signed in 1983. Total trade in goods and services is now more than $16 billion per annum. New Zealand is Australia's fifth-largest market, taking 6.6 per cent of our exports. Australia is New Zealand's most important trading partner. Total two-way investment is almost $34 billion. More than half of Australia's total investment in New

---

[127] Ibid., p.240
[128] Ibid., p.237
[129] Ibid., p.237
[130] Vaile, Hon. Mark, "*Australia-New Zealand CER Still a Benchmark 20 Years On*," Media Release, 27 March 2003 - MVT24/2003

Zealand is direct investment, reflecting the high level of economic integration that CER has achieved."[131]

Whether or not the ANZCERTA treaty is a useful template for trade liberalization is a point that may be debatable. Nevertheless, it stands as being the most successful and productive trade agreement between two Commonwealth jurisdictions to date. For this reason alone, it offers some lessons in the design and implementation of a CFTA.

## The Cairns Group

Formed in 1986, the Cairns Group is comprised of 17 agricultural exporting countries, accounting for over 30 per cent of global agricultural exports. Figuring prominently among its ranks are Commonwealth members such as Australia, Canada, New Zealand, and South Africa. Indeed, the group takes its name from the Australian town where the founding conference took place, and that nation's Agriculture Minister has chaired its subsequent meetings.

The Group's stated position is to work towards "achieving a fair and market-oriented agricultural trading system."[132] More specifically, this means "deep cuts to all tariffs (including tariff peaks) and removal of tariff escalation, the elimination of all trade-distorting domestic subsidies; the elimination of export subsidies and clear rules to prevent circumvention of export subsidy commitments."[133] This, however, is advocated with the proviso that there be "support for the principle of special and differential

---

[131] Ibid.,, 27 March 2003
[132] The Cairns Group – Vision Statement, http://www.cairnsgroup.org/vision_statement.html, 2004 August 20
[133] Ibid., 2004 August 20

treatment for developing countries (including least developed countries and small states)."[134]

The task, however, is daunting. Among OECD countries, the level of agricultural support in 1997 amounted to US$280 billion - far in excess of the total GDP for many Commonwealth states. Also, as the Cairns Group's work is focused on the negotiations within the WTO, this means the Group is inevitably caught between the two largest sources of these subsidies - the United States and the EU.

Andrew Cooper neatly summarizes the position of the Group's members as follows:

> *"What induced a feeling of solidarity among the Cairns Group was their common vulnerability in the international political economy. All of the members had suffered considerable damage from both the CAP and the EC's export restitution policy on the one side, and the United States' 'fight fire with fire' responses on the other."*[135]

As Ian Taylor explains, "in entering its dialogue with Brussels and Washington over global agricultural trade, the Cairns Group has sought to act as a bridge-builder between the developed and developing world and has attempted to present a non-confrontational face at the many negotiations it has engaged in."[136] Taylor added "it can surely not be a coincidence that in pursuing this tack the leading members of the Group - Australia, Canada and

---

[134] Ibid., 2004 August 20
[135] Cooper, Andrew, "*In Between Countries - Australia, Canada and the Search for Order in Agricultural Trade*," McGill-Queen's University Press, Montreal, 1997, p.116
[136] Taylor, Ian, "*The Cairns Group and the Commonwealth: Bridge-Building for International Trade*," The Round Table #355 (2000), p.384

South Africa - are all Commonwealth nations and are following a tradition of Commonwealth persuasive diplomacy."[137]

Such is the challenge to the Cairns Group - mediating a common ground between the world's largest trading jurisdictions where neither side seems prepared to concede any ground whatsoever. When one considers that the rules of the WTO almost demand an agreement from both America and Europe, then the road ahead seems even more difficult to traverse. Dr Michael Cullen, New Zealand's Minister of Finance, had commented to *The Economist* in 1999 that "We are a country with a large dependence on agricultural-based exports, a small isolated country not hugely strategically significant to anybody else. There is a serious risk that in a world of bilateral and regional partnerships and rivalries, we may find ourselves in a peculiarly difficult position. It would take a lot of effort on our part to avoid that possible outcome."[138]

This is not to say that the work of the Cairns Group is without success. By its own admission, it has "had more influence and impact on the agriculture negotiations than any individual members could have had independently."[139] It has also done so within a forum that brings together nations "across language, cultural and geographic boundaries."[140] Nevertheless, in waiting for progress within the WTO, the Cairns Group is waiting for two trade powerhouses, whose total combined GDP exceeds US$20 trillion, to end their stalemate.

---

[137] Ibid., p.384
[138] "*An interview with Michael Cullen*," The Economist, Oct 1, 2003, www.economist.com
[139] The Cairns Group, http://www.cairnsgroup.org/introduction.html, 2004 August 20
[140] Ibid., 2004 August 20

It is important to single out the efforts of the Cairns Group for two reasons. First, it is a solid example of how Commonwealth nations of diverse interests can cooperate – not only among themselves, but with other like-minded nations as well. Secondly, any reading or interpretation of global trade relations will inform that agriculture is both the most contentious and the most important issue within the WTO, and in other trade forums. Farm subsidies constitute the crux of the trade disagreements between the US and the EU. Moreover, as agriculture is the largest industry in most poorer nations - and by extension, its output constitutes the lion's share of potential export products to the outside world – a stalemate in this sector has a magnified effect throughout the global economy.

It is worth considering what the potential impact of a CFTA would be on world agricultural trade. As we can see, three of the four developed economies in the Commonwealth are members of the Cairns Group, and, by extension, are committed to freer access to markets. The UK, as a member of the European Union, is the notable exception. This, however, presumes that Britain supports the European position, and that Brussels truly reflects the national interests of the UK. Some anecdotal reading of official and private opinion in Britain would indicate that if the UK were free to stake out an independent position, it would not necessarily continue to accept the EU consensus as is.

Indeed, many critics of EU agricultural policy are themselves drawn from the British farming sector. They see a Common Agricultural Policy (CAP) that takes up, by many estimates, one-third of the EU's entire budget, and redistributes it to farmers on the continent – primarily in France, where the farm lobby is a potent political force. They also see that whatever reforms are undertaken, those economies will find their way not to the UK, but to extending the CAP to the Union's newer members, such as Poland.

Even if we presume, however, that Britain is committed to the letter and spirit of the CAP, this still leaves the entire remaining membership of the Commonwealth, either as members of the Cairns Group, or supportive of its objectives.

It may be one of the greatest ironies that the one sector that defies agreement or resolution at the WTO happens to be a sector where Commonwealth states speak with near unanimity. It is not inconceivable that the first major milestone of a CFTA would be an agreement that has eluded the WTO, and its GATT predecessor, for at least four decades. Such a settlement would be the moment that gives a CFTA real credibility, and provides its members with the most important breakthrough in world trade. It would also give an incentive to other members in the WTO to end the logjam once and for all.

The creation of a CFTA could be considered, in many respects, the catalyst for an agreement on global agricultural trade, and the fulfillment of the aims and the objectives of the Cairns Group.

## Chapter 8

## CFTA ORGANIZATION

As previously indicated, the unique history and past relationship between Commonwealth nations, coupled with the natural desire of sovereign peoples to maintain their independence, presents a challenge in designing an association. Rather than engage in "institution-building" and bureaucratic layering, the CFTA must be effective in its stated tasks, while still maintaining the highest level of responsiveness to member states.

The CFTA governance, therefore, would be invested in a single body, comprised of the Heads of Government of member states. Meeting on an annual basis, it would set the basic policy for the Association. Each member would exercise a single vote, with no vetoes afforded.

A Permanent Delegation, meeting on a more frequent basis, would be comprised of ambassadors and heads of delegations, as well as officials sent from member states (e.g.: Secretaries of State). This body would be responsible for discussion and review of CFTA activities, trade policy, and dispute resolution.

To assist the delegates in their negotiations and deliberations, and to ensure continuity, a permanent administrative office, the CFTA Secretariat, would be established. While centred at the headquarters of the organization, it may operate branch offices elsewhere, subject to the approval of the Permanent Delegation.

The Secretariat's functions would include supplying technical support for the Ministerial Conference, the Permanent Delegation, and its committees, analyzing trade within the CFTA, as well as outside the organization, including the promotion of the affairs of the CFTA to the general public and the media.

Unlike its WTO counterpart, the CFTA Secretariat would be required to judge applications for membership to be acceptable or not. A negative report must also include a remedial action plan, timeframes for action, as well as consultative resources to work with applicant states should they choose to accept.

The regulatory powers of the CFTA would be confined solely to compliance to the Association Charter, with penalties ranging from fines, to suspension of voting privileges, to termination of membership in the CFTA. To avoid manipulation and bias, it is further recommended that this judicial function be invested in the Secretariat, or exist as a separate, permanent committee.

In terms of budgetary requirements, the final amount would be contingent on several factors, including staffing and physical resources required. Using the WTO as a benchmark, the annual budget to maintain that organization's Secretariat of approximately 500 staff at its Geneva headquarters is roughly 122 million Swiss francs per annum.[141]

While the costs would be allocated to participating member states, it could be ameliorated partially through the use of existing resources, including the sharing of occupancy at the headquarters of the Commonwealth Secretariat at Marlborough House, London.

Indeed, that sharing of resources would eliminate duplication of research services, as much of the economic and social statistics obtained by the Commonwealth Secretariat could be applied for CFTA purposes. Moreover, it may be more expedient for the CFTA to contract specific projects to the Secretariat. CFTA staff would still be required, however, to provide the specific analysis of the data, and the recommendations needed for actioning. It could, however, reduce the need for many overheads by piggybacking upon the research and policy capacity of international organizations such as OECD, UN bodies and the World Bank.

In conjunction with this, any economies realized could be reinvested by way of the establishment of 'national offices' in member states. Not only could these offices offer a liaison service to national governments, but they could also act as a vital contact point for private actors, such as corporations and individual investors requesting specific information on the CFTA and business opportunities that may arise.

---

[141] World Trade Organization, www.wto.org, 2004 August 20

To some extent, this occurs already. In recent years, the Commonwealth Secretariat, through its Trade and Investment Access Facility (TIAF) programme, has sought to alleviate some of the inequities that affect how successful developing members are in asserting their interests in the WTO.

It is, of course, conceivable to suggest that should all members of the Commonwealth become signatories to the CFTA, that a merger of the two organizations take place. In this instance, one could foresee the CFTA emerge as a "Trade Directorate" within the larger Commonwealth Secretariat.

The calculus for such a decision, however, hinges on the confidence of member states that this would not lead to political harmonization and the imposition of a supra-national state structure. The more likely course of action would be to pursue synergies where possible, but to avoid a complete merge altogether.

This, of course, raises the bigger issue of how the day-to-day functions of a CFTA will translate for member states. Indeed, as Amrita Narlikar points out, developing states are unable to effectively promote their positions at the WTO through lack of resources, both human and information.[142] While no one can offer an iron clad guarantee that any participant nation will not feel aggrieved by the process at any particular time, certain procedures can be built into the architecture which would allow for some measure of balance.

First, a procedural directive can be put into place that would require delegations to table information and research with the Secretariat. This, in

---

[142] Narlikar, Amrita, "*The Politics of Participation*," The Round Table #364 (2002).

turn, would be made available to all delegations through a secure Intranet. Exceptions could be allowed for, including national security and defense considerations. Also, this requirement would be deemed necessary only for evidentiary information intended for use in a debate or vote. Delegations would not be required to divulge information up and above the issue being discussed. Conversely, no delegation would be permitted to introduce 'evidence' without a prior disclosure to the Permanent Delegation, in its role as the Committee of the Whole.

In terms of the physical demands on national delegations, while not at first, it is conceivable that a growth in both membership and the scope of the agreement will create a situation analogous to that we have seen at the WTO.

While it is clear that the relative positions of potential CFTA members would create advantages and disadvantages among individual missions, it would be unwise to place a cap, or limit, or any one member's representation – either in terms of numbers or budgetary resources. It would be, in effect, a subjugation of national sovereignty, as well as a statutory requirement for governments to betray their sworn duty to uphold the national interest. In addition, if the aforementioned rules on disclosure are put in place, it limits the potential resources of the CFTA as a whole.

One compromise worth considering would be a proxy voting system. Nations seeking to exercise their vote, or comment, on a given issue, but cannot do so for reasons of scheduling or mission resources, would be allowed to have another member vote their proxy. In this instance, a member state need only reach an agreement with another like-minded delegation who would be prepared to carry out the physical request.

As matters of courtesy and privilege, it would be recommended that the intent to invoke a proxy, either to delegate to, or use on behalf of, a member be declared in advance. Furthermore, no member state could exercise more than one national proxy on any particular vote, and that the proxy would be confined to one vote, the exception being where that same agenda item required multiple ballots.

One additional requirement for proxy voting should be the inclusion of a Statement of Intent from the member whose vote is being represented. It is not enough for one country to simply cast another's ballot – even if it has been negotiated and duly agreed. The absent member must provide a brief statement outlining that delegation's position and the reasons why they are voting either in the affirmative or the negative. The ambassador of the country voting the proxy would be required to read that statement in open committee and subsequently table it with the Secretariat.

If one presumes the vitality of a CFTA, as well as the desirability of membership, then the organization will need to be creative in its approaches to decision-making and representation. It is of vital importance that the rules that govern a CFTA provide outcomes that are as free of undue bias as is possible. Only by striving to this objective can an association be engendered with the degree of confidence needed to thrive.

## Chapter 9

## QUALIFICATIONS FOR MEMBERSHIP

If a CFTA is to be, in any way, successful in its goal of increasing trade, commerce, and investment within the Commonwealth, an appreciation of how wealth is generated must be apparent.

History and economics show that successful economies within a closed society with no democratic ethos are the exception, not the rule. Creating wealth in those circumstances usually involves huge dislocations and major commitments to a 'command economy,' where resources are allocated based on regime prerogatives, not societal need.

Pierre Pettigrew, Canada's Minister for International Trade, observed that "the combination of balance and dynamism that has been central to the…approach has also been, in my view, at the heart of the extraordinary miracle of progress, because development remains the exception on our planet. This miracle was made possible by the constructive "tandem" of the state and the market... Indeed, highly developed markets would not even exist if there had not been a state to guarantee property rights and other individual rights in this very country."[143]

Any objective reading of the history of the 20th Century compels one to appreciate the relationship between economic and personal freedom. It is only through the development of democracy and civil society, where a nation is allowed to develop and nurture its talent. It is also only under these conditions that investors have the confidence to invest capital and anticipate that their investment is assured, let alone that it will yield a dividend.

While a CFTA should be in no way a supra-national structure, or a device for imposing political institutions extraterritorially, there must be a set of minimum standards by which all members are required to conduct themselves. Rather than a means of 'controlling' a nation, these rules must be designed with the sole purpose of guaranteeing the integrity of the relationship.

The preconditions for candidate states would focus on the conditions necessary for participation to be of benefit to that state and the CFTA as a whole. They would include the following, and would be enshrined in the CFTA Charter:

- The right to private property;

---

[143] Pettigrew, Hon. Pierre, *"Reconciling the Spirit and Ethics of Liberalism in the 21st Century"*, Trade Policy Research 2003, (Ottawa: Minister of Public Works and Government Services Canada), 2003, p.vii

- The right of personal liberty against abuses of power, crime, and corruption;

- Enforcement of the rights of contract;

- Stable political administration conducted by publicly known rules;

- Provision of responsive and democratic government

Upon receipt of an application from a candidate state, the CFTA Secretariat would undertake a detailed investigation, including field research and monitoring, to establish whether these preconditions have actually been met. It would be the task of the teams to conduct their researches without any actions that could be seen as prejudicial one way or the other. The style of inquiry would be observational, similar to that employed by those who serve on observer teams to national elections. Using a set of criteria predetermined before the review, CFTA field researchers would be called upon to offer an assessment as to how well a candidate has scored on the preset benchmarks.

As previously mentioned, the assets and experience of the Commonwealth Secretariat would be invaluable to the performance of this task.

If an affirmative report has been received, the report would be forwarded to the Permanent Delegation for debate and actioning. If a report is in the negative, the CFTA Secretariat would be required to publish its dissenting report, making it available to both the Permanent Delegation, as well as the government of the applicant state.

As membership in the CFTA would become increasingly beneficial to member states, the price of contravening any of its founding principles would also become very costly. Adherence to a basic charter, therefore, becomes a potent tool in encouraging free and fair trade, as well as human rights and the primacy of law. Flagrant abuses such as those carried out by the Mugabe government in Zimbabwe would be punished by a suspension of trade - a huge blow to any government's attempts to generate revenue and develop the local economy.

In forming a CFTA, however, the right of legitimate national self-determination must be respected. Many Commonwealth nations still harbor long and deep resentments from their colonial pasts. It is important, therefore, that the foundations be based on equality and respect. Member states will be asked to observe a Charter of Conduct, which they are free to accept, or reject. Acceptance means unfettered access, while rejection means lack thereof.

It is conceivable that a leader, or a regime, would calculate that the benefits of their actions outweigh the potential risks and would proceed to abuse their authority. The CFTA's response must be to cut off the resources supplied to such a regime, but not so far as to create an undue hardship to CFTA based enterprises, or those citizens of that nation whose financial well-being depends on such exchanges.

Toward this end, an effective remedy would be to partially suspend the benefits of membership. This may mean restoring tariffs and duties to their original level, or introducing a temporary duty that would be directed to a specific reserve fund, to be administered at the discretion of the CFTA. The monies may be used to support civil society efforts in that particular state, be used to service their existing debt repayments, be held and invested until such time as that state has undertaken the reforms necessary for readmission, or a combination of these alternatives.

Restoring tariffs and duties to pre-CFTA levels is but one step. It must be also followed with strong representations to other multilateral organizations such as the United Nations. Also, the commitment to restore CFTA privileges must be made contingent on a restoration of democracy and civil society.

It would be up to the leadership of a particular nation to ensure that the minimum qualifications are met and maintained. That being said, if a nation has been able to maintain these systemic reforms, and the benefits of increased trade and access to capital have been accrued for a sufficient period of time, civil society becomes resilient enough to withstand a return to less democratic practices. As Pierre Pettigrew remarked, "for confidence to continue to be the engine of progress, we have to make sure that it is accompanied by an ethic of conscience. The two must go hand-in-hand; our system requires that the public conscience be respected."[144]

In the end, however, if a CFTA is to function in such a way as to strike the right balance between national sovereignty and multilateral cohesion, it is imperative that the rights and obligations of membership are understood.

---

[144] Pettigrew, Hon. Pierre, *"Reconciling the Spirit and Ethics of Liberalism in the 21st Century"*, in Trade Policy Research 2003, (Ottawa: Minister of Public Works and Government Services Canada), 2003, p. viii

Clear and simple rules that address basic human rights and freedoms are imperative to establish a standard of conduct that benefits the flow of trade, reduces poverty and is sensitive to local customs and cultural standards. Simple rules mean ease of compliance, but they also mean the absence of excuses for not observing them.

## Chapter 10

## CFTA IMPLEMENTATION

The establishment of any legal framework between nations implies two criteria: first, that there is a desire to enter such an agreement based on the perceived benefit; and second, that each party has confidence in the other signatories to fulfill their obligations.

It would be fair to assume that the first criterion could be met easily and immediately. The benefits of freer trade for economies, and citizens are well documented and evident.

The second criterion, however, presents a challenge to potential CFTA signatories, as political, economic and legal regimes in some candidate states do not easily lend themselves to an immediate involvement in a CFTA.

As with the experience with the Lomé Conventions, the greater, and more immediate, success in implementing free trade agreements depends less on the relative size and maturity of the economy and more on the political, judicial and social underpinnings of it.

Openness and democracy equal economic stability, and that stability is key to successful relations in matters of trade. For that reason, and the broader goal of a CFTA, it must be a non-negotiable requirement for membership. As Sir Shridath Ramphal asserted "There must be effective multilateralism, more shared responsibilities, less paranoia about sovereignty, more genuine acceptance of the idea of global society. In short, globalization must not run ahead of global governance or it will become like wild horses un-harnessed from the chariot of human good."[145]

This is not to say that one should view this possible initiative as a means of usurping the power and authority of sovereign states. What it does mean is that the CFTA have a clear, coherent, limited Charter that binds participant states only to the extent necessary as to ensure its objective – free trade among members.

Multilateralism, thankfully enough, does not presume any particular orthodoxy in its structures. There is no specified formula for how much harmonization must occur between nations partnered together. Both NAFTA and the EU, for example, are free trade blocs, and yet both have pursued their development in very dissimilar ways. There are, granted, advantages and disadvantages to either approach. The important point,

---

[145] Ramphal, Sir Shridath, "*Global Governance or a New Imperium: Which is it to be?,*" The Round Table (2003), #369, p.215

however, is that the quality and character of an organization must reflect the philosophy of its members, and be a suitable vehicle for their expression.

Ideally, all nations of the Commonwealth would offer a serious bid for participation. In the absence of all states having met the initial preconditions, however, it would be advised to begin with a core group that is able to meet those standards immediately. Not only does this begin the process of creating a functioning association, but it also provides an incentive to those wishing to join.

It is proposed that the CFTA membership and expansion be conducted in four distinct phases:

Phase 1 would see the creation of an initial grouping of four nations – Australia, Canada, New Zealand, and the United Kingdom. This group represents the most affluent and industrialized economies of the Commonwealth. Combined with stable political, judicial and social institutions, their ability to quickly integrate into a CFTA is vitally important if the organization is to have the ability to expand and succeed.

Based on 1999 World Bank estimates, the combined GDP of the CFTA at this phase would be roughly US$3 trillion, making it the world's third largest free trade zone – behind NAFTA and the European Union. This gives the CFTA, at this stage, the critical mass needed to move forward.

Phase 2 expansion of the CFTA would occur after the structural framework of the organization was firmly in place, and when eligible states were ready to complete negotiations. This phase would focus on linking regional centers of power, such as Singapore (ASEAN), Commonwealth members of the CARICOM group, and the Republic of South Africa

(Southern Africa Customs Union), and would allow the organization the ability to build the framework necessary for further growth.

Phase 3 would, in many ways, be the most ambitious phase for expansion, as it would see the largest per capita growth in the organization. In this round, India, Pakistan, Malaysia, and southern African states would be invited to join, subject to qualification. Phase 4 would consist of admitting remaining Commonwealth nations that would qualify under the terms of the Charter.

While there is no suggested time frame for such expansion, it will be important to pursue this growth with a mind toward the issues and challenges that are commensurate with welcoming new members. As we will discuss in further detail, allowing some developing states the opportunity to thrive and benefit from CFTA participation means an emphasis on issues of development and offering tangible encouragement of a civil society.

Beyond the last phase of membership growth, the CFTA may consider associate status to non-Commonwealth nations that meet the eligibility criteria, and are approved by the CFTA. Furthermore, the CFTA might, collectively, approve free trade agreements with other economic players, such as the United States, the European Union, or the People's Republic of China (PRC). Individual may find it advantageous to use the collective bargaining strength of the Association to negotiate agreements beyond.

Should a CFTA be established, the decision as to what states would qualify for admittance would be subject to much debate and to factors unforeseen in this essay. It can only be hoped that when such decisions are made, they reflect the political and economic realities of integrating states into such a trading regime.

## Chapter 11

## CFTA AND DEVELOPMENT AID

When one looks to the potential membership of a CFTA, it becomes exceedingly clear that developmental assistance will become a major issue. Many questions will need to be addressed – how much, to whom, for what purposes, and under what conditions?

Aid for developing nations is an exceedingly complex issue that touches upon every facet of a society – its political, judicial and social structures, as well as its history and its place in the global community. There are many schools of thought, and no quick answers.

While in its initial phase, a CFTA will not be in need of such mechanisms, subsequent expansion will assert the issue.

If a CFTA is successful in reducing, or eliminating tariffs and duties, it is not inconceivable that benefits would accrue immediately to its developing members. A review of trade statistics reveals the following picture:

- south to north payments are four times greater than north to north payments;

- south-to-south payments are the largest, accounting for 42 percent of the world total;

- 71 percent of the developing country tariff payments go to other developing countries; and

- The effective duty rate paid by small developing countries is often far higher than that paid by industrial countries[146]

It would be naïve to presume that the benefits of CFTA membership, and the systemic reforms needed to secure it, would be enough to transform a nation and a society. Access to CFTA markets provides the means to generate wealth, and reform ensures that it is not squandered or misappropriated. These factors are important preconditions, but we must

---

[146] Curtis, John M., and Ciuriak, Dan, "*Towards Half Time in the Doha Development Agenda*", in Trade Policy Research 2003, (Ottawa: Minister of Public Works and Government Services Canada), 2003, p.24

recognize that more resources will be needed to wrest these nations from their state of inertia.

The current state of many Commonwealth nations speaks to the enormity of the task:

- One-third of the Commonwealth's population lives on less than US$1 a day;

- Around 60 per cent of global HIV cases are in the Commonwealth;

- Nearly 60 per cent of the Commonwealth citizens lack access to essential drugs and adequate sanitation facilities while some 270 million of its people lack access to improved water supplies;

- Around half of the world's 115 million children who are without access to primary school live in the Commonwealth.

- Young people constitute over 50 per cent of the Commonwealth population and a large percentage of them are adversely affected by unemployment, poverty, HIV/AIDS and illiteracy.[147]

---

[147] Abdullah, Saiful Azhar "*Rough Waters ahead for the Commonwealth*," Business Times, Kuala Lumpur, Dec. 10, 2003, p.24

Structural reforms within political institutions, and the encouragement of a thriving civil society, of course, are only part of the needed response – albeit a crucial part.

If one presumes that the aforementioned reforms have been, to any extent, successful in their objectives, then two major problems yet remain – external debt loads and access to capital where the costs are proportionate to the ability to pay.

Good government costs money. It requires adequate resources to finance the infrastructure necessary to provide vital services such as health care, education, water and sanitation. As Dr. Kaire M. Mbuende states "Countries of Eastern and Southern Africa can only derive maximum benefits from the conclusion of [trade agreements] if the supply side constraints are addressed comprehensively. These constraints include poor infrastructures, lack of access to inexpensive power and water and shortage of skilled manpower which was further exacerbated by the HIV/AIDS pandemic."[148]

Moreover, the good maintenance of civil society requires a 'knowledge infrastructure', particularly the means to provide essential communications and information networks to the populace. As the global economy develops into an 'information economy', the ability to compete will reflect as much on the creation and dissemination of knowledge and new technologies as it does in traditional manufacturing and production. The following table illustrates the comparison of this asset in selected Commonwealth countries:

---

[148] Mbuende, Dr. Kaire M., "*ACP-EU Future Trade Relations: Challenges and Opportunities for Eastern and Southern African Countries*," in Commonwealth Trade Hot Topics, Issue No. 15, p.6

Newspapers, Radio, Television, Telephones, and Computers, by selected countries (rates per 1,000 persons)[149]

| Country | Daily Newspaper Circulation (1996) | Radios (1997) | Televisions (1997) | Telephone main lines (2000) | Cell Phone Customers (2000) | Personal Computers (2000) |
|---|---|---|---|---|---|---|
| Australia | 296 | 1391 | 554 | 524 | 446 | 465 |
| Canada | 158 | 1067 | 710 | 654 | 225 | 390 |
| India | n.a. | 120 | 65 | 32 | 4 | 5 |
| New Zealand | 216 | 997 | 512 | 496 | 366 | 360 |
| Sierra Leone | n.a | n.a | n.a | n.a | n.a | n.a |
| South Africa | 34 | 355 | 134 | 125 | 120 | 62 |
| UK | 331 | 1443 | 521 | 567 | 670 | 338 |

As developing nations attempt to deal with the burden of external debt, the outflows of capital curtail their ability to finance infrastructure projects and government services – monies to raise living standards and gain greater economic competitiveness.

---

[149] Sources: Except as noted, newspaper, radio, and television – United Nations Educational, Scientific, and Cultural Organization, Paris, France, Statistical Yearbook (copyright); telephones, cellular phones, and personal computers – International Telecommunications Union, Geneva, Switzerland, World Telecommunications Indicators.

It may be worthy to consider that the CFTA develop a mechanism under which poorer members may be able to service or refinance existing debts. Both Canadian Prime Minister Paul Martin and Britain's Chancellor of the Exchequer, Gordon Brown, have advocated, within the context of the International Monetary Fund (IMF), a, 'Emergency Standstill Clause', where "in the event of a crisis, and where a country adopts good policies, it may be prepared to sanction temporary debt standstills, by lending into arrears, in order to enable countries to reach agreements with creditors on debt rescheduling. By making this clear in advance, private lenders would know that in future crises they would be expected to contribute to the solution as part of any IMF-led rescue."[150] It would be, in effect, "a cooling off period consistent with contractual obligations."[151]

Other possible strategies may include forgiving interest accrued, or a portion of the principal, extending the term of repayment, or offering a preferred rate of interest. Taken separately, or in conjunction, these devices can help reduce debt burdens for a nation. When combined with increases in national GDP, these countries may be able to accelerate the process of reducing their total debt.

In terms of access to capital, reliance on markets in the beginning will not allow for the accelerated growth needed. The private sector in poorer CFTA states will need the services of an institution that can respond to these unique circumstances.

---

[150] Brown, Rt. Hon. Gordon, "*New Global Structures for the New Global Age*," The Round Table (1999), #349, p.49

[151] Martin, Rt. Hon. Paul "*Canada and the Commonwealth Business Forum*," The Round Table (1999), #349, p.37

Further to this, it is recommended that a Commonwealth Development Bank be established to provide financing for private sector businesses and governments for specific infrastructure projects, such as health and education facilities, or transportation, communications and energy grids.

The capital for such a lender would be provided by donor members who would also comprise its board of directors. Having said this, it may be desirable to set aside a minority representation on a board for recipient states. They would, however, be prevented from assuming the Chairmanship or any executive duties.

The advantage of assuming such a management structure would be to strike a balance between the requirements of donor members to have accountability in the management of the funds they provide with the necessity of client members to articulate both their need and their practical challenges in development. Through this synthesis of perspectives, one would hope to see a position that dispenses with the often adversarial relationships indicative of development aid and financing partnerships. One might see an emphasis on fiscal accountability twinned with initiatives that meet more tangible needs in local societies.

One particular question arises about the status of loans and government financing to members who are suspended from the CFTA for contravening the Charter. Logically, one realizes that 'calling in' these loans is a practical impossibility. Such a move could needlessly aggravate the economic conditions of a people beyond what is necessary. Furthermore, any overtly aggressive or heavy-handed approach could lead to a more entrenched attitude from both sides. The CFTA, however, would have a responsibility to take a principled stand.

It would, therefore, be wise to propose that upon the suspension of CFTA membership, all debt held by the CFTA, or its members, would not qualify for relief of principal or a reduced interest accrual. The CFTA would be obliged to raise the interest rate on such debt to the level consistent with other global lenders, such as the World Bank and the International Monetary Fund (IMF). Furthermore, there would be no opportunity to renegotiate terms or engage in new borrowing. The exception to this rule would be private-sector borrowing.

Such an approach, albeit imperfect, is a practical means of squaring the economic relations of member states with the responsibility to proactively promote the minimum standards of CFTA conduct.

None of this discussion, however, covers the existing activities of the Commonwealth Secretariat and its colloraries. CFTA activities would be a compliment to, and not a replacement for, existing activities within the Secretariat. Indeed, one could see the work of the two structures acting as part of a continuum. The Secretariat would aid and assist Commonwealth states in undertaking the measures necessary for qualification for CFTA membership. Beyond this, the CFTA would be able to apply more specific assistance programs geared toward development and economic reform.

Again, it is important to bear in mind that there is no universal template for constructing international agreements. The past century has seen much dialogue and 'institution building' take place, but the organizations that were borne of these labours reflect the sensitivities of the participants, as well as the specific tasks they were designed for.

Trade agreements have, to this point, had a very mixed record regarding issues of development. Indeed, this seems to be the main point of contention with those who style themselves as critics of globalization. But while the problems of globalization have been, more or less, accurately defined, the blame has not. If trade agreements do not effectively address issues of development, it is because they were designed to eliminate trade barriers, not enable development. Where the WTO has responded to this agenda, it has either been as a happy coincidence, or due to political pressures that are unavoidable. In many ways, getting the WTO to develop a comprehensive strategy on this issue is rather like using the family automobile to haul a ton of granite, then complaining that it does not work as well as a dump truck.

Prime Minister Martin of Canada, speaking within the current context of IMF activities toward the developing world, observed that what was needed was "...a renewed commitment to strong policy foundations by the emerging market economies."[152] He added "without good domestic policy on their part, no amount of effort by the international community is going to prevent periodic financial problems or promote sustained growth. Good policy, though, does not necessarily mean one size fits all. Off-the-shelf solutions more often than not are simply an inadequate response to complex problems. IMF programs in troubled economies clearly need to be tailored to local conditions."[153]

A proper job requires the proper tools. If a CFTA is to participate in issues pertaining to development, as well as trade, then member states will need to specifically define that role, as well as the parameters within which it will function. Indeed, responding to the development agenda will have to be 'hard wired' into the CFTA structure.

---

[152] Martin, Rt. Hon. Paul, "*Canada and the Commonwealth Business Forum*," The Round Table #349 (1999), p.35
[153] Martin, Rt. Hon. Paul, "*Canada and the Commonwealth Business Forum*," p.35

Paul Martin observed "as history has shown, however, open markets are the best mechanism we have for allocating resources in individual economies and across national borders. Therefore, the task that faces policy makers is not simply to lament the inefficiencies of global financial markets, but urgently to find ways to make them work better. After all, that is what we have done at home. No one, not even the most libertarian of us I would hope, believes that the free market should be a free for all."[154]

That, however, will not be the challenge. The tougher task will be to make sure that this duty is compatible with the other priorities of trade liberalization and upholding national sovereignty. How well this balancing act is achieved will depend upon the intelligence and the imagination of those charged with the organizations very creation. The judgment of success or failure will belong to those who measure the transformative effects of those policies, whether they live up to their expectations of lifting societies, or whether it merely becomes the latest in a series of international constructs that gets written off as a good intention and nothing more. Gordon Brown summarized that challenge when he commented:

> *"The partnership between the Commonwealth countries is an indispensible foundation of international stability and prosperity. Never in all of economic history have so many depended so much on genuine economic co-operation among all the nations of the world. Our shared commitment to open trade and orderly progress has been a driving force for growth in all our countries - even in countries that not so long ago seemed likely to be permanently left behind."*[155]

---

[154] Martin, Rt. Hon. Paul, *"Canada and the Commonwealth Business Forum,"* p.34
[155] Brown, Rt. Hon. Gordon, *"New Global Structures for the New Global Age,"* The Round Table (1999), #349, p.39

Whatever the response ends up being, it is clear that both sides in this debate have much to bring to the table, and that the answer lies in some form of a synthesis of the two perspectives. Given the current situation within many multilateral fora, it is clear that this will only happen under a new 'architecture', one that a CFTA can very well provide.

*Chapter 12*

CFTA AND THE UNITED STATES

As indicated, two of the distinguishing features of Commonwealth states are the widespread usage of the English language, and a legal system based on English common law. We have also seen that such shared traits allow for a comparative advantage in trade and commerce. We have also recognized the fact that developed members of a CFTA will need to provide the necessary muscle to assist in the transformation of its poorer members' economies.

Some may argue that if these are the challenges and opportunities before a CFTA, then a logical step forward would be to extend the offer of full membership to the United States. Indeed, proponents of what has become known as the 'Anglosphere' have already advocated such goals. Champions of this idea come from both sides of the Atlantic, and from both the US and the Commonwealth. Former British Prime Minister, Baroness Thatcher, and

Canadian publishing magnate, Lord Black, have both advocated Britain's removal from the European Union in order to join the NAFTA. Also, commentators such as James C. Bennett and John O'Sullivan have synthesized the idea of a broader coalition of nations sharing the aforementioned attributes combining into an informal "network Commonwealth."

These ideas have much currency in certain circles in London, Washington and other Commonwealth capitals at present. In the opinion of the author, this school of thought does bring an added dimension to the question of wither Commonwealth Free Trade. At its heart, it bases its validity on the same criteria as the proposal of a CFTA, and its aspirations are similar in scope and portent. The difference between a CFTA and the Anglosphere school – if it can be called a difference – is in how it casts a potential relationship between a CFTA and the United States. That is, while the Anglosphere movement does not dictate any particular model for US-Commonwealth relations, this proposal does.

In considering the history of American foreign and trade policy, and the political forces that shape it, one must recognize that if a formal relationship between the two is to exist, it must be based on a particular structure that does not set up irreconcilable tensions that would imperil the cohesion of a CFTA. One can be supportive of cooperation between the US and Commonwealth states, but the inherent political cultures on both sides will predetermine success or failure. Concerns boil down to just one point – how do nations within the 'Anglosphere' define multilateralism and international cooperation? On this one, extremely important, point, one will find that within the Anglosphere, the United States is a nation truly set apart.

Students of American foreign policy will be quick to recognize a theme that has been present since their War of Independence and the first sittings of the Continental Congress in the 1780's. Scholars often refer to the phenomenon as the notion of 'American exceptionalism.'

This notion holds that the United States, in its struggle to become what we now know as the world's first western liberal democracy, is a nation set apart. Being the first nation to establish a democracy under these particular specifications, there has been a recurring idea that the extension of these political values beyond its borders is not only a mission, but a sacred responsibility. This idea is well seated in the American social and political consciousness, as Walter LaFeber explains:

> *"Americans…have viewed their secular, or more earthly, successes as part of a higher purpose…From their beginnings, they have justified developing a continent and then much of the globe simply by saying they were spreading the principles of civilization as well as making profit. They have had no problem seeing their prosperity – indeed, their rise from a sparsely settled continent to the world's superpower – as part of a Higher Purpose or, as it was known during much of their history, a Manifest Destiny."*[156]

Indeed, two of the phrases that currently enjoy currency among some foreign policy scholars in the United States – *"Pax Americana"* and a new *"American Century"* are not new. The former phrase was coined by Charles Evans Hughes, a Secretary of State, and Republican Presidential nominee in

---

[156] LaFeber, Walter, *"The American Age,"* (New York: W.W. Norton and Company), 1994, p. 5

1916[157]; while the latter was the title of a book written by Time Magazine publisher Henry Luce in 1941.[158]

The result of this history and political culture is the creation of a foreign policy – indeed, a world view – that allows for cooperation and consensus under only the most specific and exacting circumstances. No country in modern history has so resolute, or has so jealously guarded this prerogative, as has the United States of America. This works well for her citizens, but the benefits may only be assured as far as the rights of that citizenship are enjoyed.

The nature of international relations and the intercourse of nation-states, however, offers no stable, self-evident models for the conduct of affairs. Nations are, by their very construct, self-interested parties that seek to enter partnerships that, at their minimum, preserve their sovereign status guaranteeing their ability to act on behalf of their people – the ultimate moral responsibility of a democracy.

Negotiations are, at their very core, the synthesis of two or more perspectives into a single, unitary direction of purpose. Where all participants accept one another with the equal status of peers, reluctant to cause or suffer injury to themselves or others, and are understanding of the necessity of ethical and principled compromise, agreements often do come into being and are viewed to be, on the whole, positive and helpful.

This is not to suggest, or to infer, that a CFTA would not respect the sovereignty of member states. Indeed, in enforcement of applicable

---

[157] LaFeber, Walter, *"The American Age,"* p.335
[158] LaFeber, Walter, *"The American Age,"* p.399

standards, most Commonwealth nations would, as history suggests, be content with 'outcome-based' remedies. That is, that the focus would be not on the specific legal and juridical remedies enacted, but whether the stated objectives have been met by them.

For example, in terms of a thriving democracy, it matters little whether a state is a constitutional monarchy or a republic; whether the legislature is unicameral or bicameral; or whether its mode of selection is 'first-past-the-post,' proportional representation (PR), a single transferable vote (SVT), or some combination thereof. What does matter is that each citizen is afforded a vote, and that vote is cast freely – without threat or coercion – and that it counts equally in the process of selecting government representatives. In many respects, the ends do justify the means – particularly when the major challenge is to find unity within such diversity.

In accepting these premises, one must recognize what can, or cannot, be guaranteed or ensured. One may guarantee that the forum of discussion is fair and relatively free of bias, or that the terms negotiated are not unduly injurious or punitive. Accepting the principles of equal status, we may presume that injury is neither intended nor accepted, lest sovereign parties remove themselves from the process.

The United States, and her leaders, understand and appreciate the need to work in concert with other nations on issues of peace and prosperity. America also appreciates the fundamental values of democracy and the rule of law.

The difficulty with the philosophy of 'American exceptionalism' is that it demands a high price for this American participation. It is a price that, quite often, impedes the natural progress of negotiation and consensus. America demands her independence, which can only be guaranteed by ensuring the outcome of any process falls to her favour as she perceives it, as interpreted by her political leaders and their constituencies.

The real issue, however, is not so much that the United States and American interests wish to control situations for the sake of power, although in some cases it may. What is really at stake is an ingrown skepticism and aversion to ideas, concepts and structures not rooted in the American tradition as it is understood by her people. That is, to say, rules and institutions not identifiable as an American creation.

American foreign policy, to the outside world, can seem quite schizophrenic. It has an honest belief in democratic values, and in working cooperatively with others. It often sees cooperation, however, in very uncooperative ways – its concept of compromise is, to some extent, in fact, very uncompromising.

Unfortunately, in any negotiation, one party may only be assured of the outcome if all others are compelled to forfeit or sacrifice their own concerns or interests. That is, what America demands from her partners can only be assured if those partners place the interests of America above their own. Given the strength and preponderance of the United States in military and economic matters, many nations have calculated that such sacrifices are the price one pays for prosperity at home.

Historically, when the United States has negotiated trade agreements, it has laboured under the view that both the ends and the means must be equally justified. That is, it is not enough to arrive at a point where one can say that trade is free and fair. The processes, as well, must be proscribed.

## *The dispute over softwood lumber*

An example of how 'free and fair trade' is often interpreted differently would be the ongoing dispute between the US and Canada over softwood lumber, particularly where it relates to the cost of cutting – the so-called 'stumpage fees.' Unlike the US, where virtually all woodlots are owned by private interests, most timber in places like British Columbia is located on government, or 'Crown' lands. American interests saw Canadian stumpage fees as being too low, making them *de facto* subsidies. American lumber producers wanted no less than the provincial governments in Canada to follow the American system and auction off timber rights at market prices.

The dispute came to a head in August 2001 when the Bush administration backed a U.S. forest industry bid to hit Canadian lumber with billions of dollars in duties. This meant that Canadians exporting south of the border were charged an 18.8 per cent countervailing duty - a tax applied to imports deemed to have been unfairly subsidized. That penalty increased two months later when Washington imposed a further anti-dumping duty that now sits at 8.4 per cent. The US argument has been that Canadian lumber has been unfairly subsidized by governments; so much, in fact, that Canadian exports account for nearly one-third of the domestic American market.

The governments of British Columbia and Canada vigorously disputed this, and immediately took their case to both NAFTA tribunals and to special panels of the WTO.

Over a period of three to four years, both NAFTA and the WTO have concluded that no evidence of predatory practices had been presented. Both have determined that the United States has failed to make their case. Despite this, rather than suspend the tariff, the US continually redrafts its case and sends it forward for yet another hearing. In fact, where the tariff is concerned, the American lumber lobby has argued that the billions of dollars paid by Canadian producers should not be returned, but divided amongst their industry members.

There have been negotiations between both countries and affected parties in order to find a resolution, but neither side seemed prepared to accept the proposals being offered. In the meantime, estimates are that 15,000 jobs were lost in British Columbia's forest industry – the province's largest industry. In 2001, U.S. Trade Ambassador Robert Zoellick stated that the trade war would continue until Canada imposed its own taxes on lumber exports, which it refused to do.[159]

The dispute came close to resolution in the summer of 2003, with the announcement of a draft agreement. It required Canada to cap lumber exports to account for 30 per cent of the U.S. market, down from 34 per cent. If the quota was exceeded, Canada would have to pay a penalty. The plan was nixed two days later when U.S. producers said "Canada needed to make more compromises."[160]

A NAFTA decision on August 13, 2003 was considered a partial victory for Canada. A panel ruled that, while the Canadian lumber industry is

---

[159] CBC News, Softwood Lumber Dispute – Backgrounder, http://www.cbc.ca/news/indepth/background/softwood_lumber.html, 2004 Aug 31.
[160] CBC News, Softwood Lumber Dispute – Backgrounder, 2004 Aug 31.

subsidized, the 18 per cent tariff imposed on softwood lumber by the United States was too high. The ruling did not throw out the duty, but it did require the U.S. Commerce Department to review its position. The report stated that the U.S. made a mistake in miscalculating its duties by basing them on U.S. prices, and by not taking Canadian market conditions into consideration. It ordered Washington to recalculate them. The decision was legally binding, and required the parties to put its decisions into effect within 60 days.

Two weeks later, a WTO panel concluded that the U.S. wrongly applied harsh duties on Canadian softwood exports. The also found that provincial stumpage programs provided a "financial benefit" to Canadian producers. But, the panel made it clear that the benefit was not enough to be a subsidy, and did not justify current U.S. duties.

One proposal offered by the US negotiators did hold out the promise of a settlement. It, however, amounted to having the government of British Columbia agree to dismantle its existing system of timber licensing in favour of those currently being used in the United States.

Essentially, a democratically elected government was being offered a lifeline to rescue its single largest industry, and export product, from jeopardy if it agreed to dismantle its own forest management policy, and accept, without question or debate, the policy and management system of a foreign country.

While the question of whether lower timber costs in British Columbia are the result of predatory pricing practices has not been answered conclusively, what is clear is that evidence of such has not been found in the nearly dozen times that NAFTA and WTO tribunals have studied the case. As yet, there is no 'smoking gun.' In fairness to both countries, the rulings of the NAFTA and WTO tribunals were not presented in a particularly helpful way, and could easily be interpreted as a win for either side. For the Americans, it was a vindication of their position that the industry was being subsidized. For Canada, it was confirmation that stumpage fees were not trade distorting, and that the US Commerce Department did not calculate the duties correctly. With both sides feeling vindicated, it is understandable why the dispute was as protracted as it was.

To outside observers, one might look at other factors that would equally impact the price differential between Canadian and US stumpage fees. One might be that Canadian lumber mills are far more efficient than their American counterparts – a point that has been put forth by Canadian industry officials. Second, the Canadian dollar has been, for many years, only worth 65 to 75 percent of its US counterpart, and that the difference in exchange rates becomes a natural discount passed on to the consumer. The third reason could simply be that Canada, being the second largest nation in the world in terms of territory, simply possesses a greater supply of trees, and that true to the economic theories of supply and demand, this would result in lower per unit costs. The same theory holds that drilling for oil in the deserts of Saudi Arabia has a lower overhead than when one drills from an offshore platform in the middle of the North Sea during the stormy season.

The lack of discussion regarding all economic factors that impact the cost of a good like softwood lumber is not, in itself, surprising. It can only serve to weaken the negotiating stance of the side that insists that stumpage fees are the only thing that determines price. Acknowledgement of a more complex economic and industrial model would, in effect, place a premium on a trade settlement over the interests of a politically strong domestic lobby.

It is for this reason that the experience of Canada – US trade in softwood lumber is particularly instructive.

*A silver lining nonetheless*

This is not to unfairly denigrate the Canada-United States trading relationship, for on the whole, it has been of great benefit to Canada. As Perrin Beatty points out "Canada's exports of goods and services to the US have grown at an average annual rate of 9.3 per cent since 1989." This meant a total of more than C$382 billion in 2003. Moreover, with reference to Canada's exports to NAFTA partner Mexico, it has grown "at an average annual rate of 14.2 per cent since 1994… to C$3.5 billion in 2002."[161]

Also, according to a Statistics Canada report "the reduction in tariffs between Canada and the U.S. under free trade boosted the odds of survival for more than two-thirds of Canadian manufacturing firms."[162] While cuts to Canadian tariffs raised risks for Canadian firms, the complimentary reductions in U.S. tariffs more than compensated for this. It was also found that "higher productivity and low debt levels shelter firms from the impact of falling tariff protection."[163]

It is, however, a cautionary tale insofar as it teaches some valuable lessons in how to resolve outstanding issues, and do so without having the results unfairly determined by the regretful axiom that "might makes right."

---

[161] Beatty, Hon. Perrin, *"Beyond NAFTA: The rules for global engagement,"* Plant Magazine, Vol. 63, Issue 1, January 19, 2004, p.23
[162] Beauchesne, Eric, Wire Feed – Business, Statistics, CanWest News Service, Don Mills, Ontario, Canada, 2004 Apr 28
[163] Ibid., 2004 Apr 28

A useful tool for a successful trade relationship - particularly with America, but not necessarily restricted to that country – is the use of binational panels, as referred to under Chapter 19 of the NAFTA agreement. Under this section, both nations may submit their dispute to a tribunal, made up of members from each party, whose decisions carry the weight of court rulings. It has been a remarkably successful mechanism for resolving disputes. Indeed, it is through such a panel that Canada has had some success on the softwood lumber issue in August of 2004.

We must remember, however, that the preference for bilateral agreements means that the legal architecture will not always translate to other FTAs signed by the United States. The dynamics of the particular relationships that America has with potential partners will certainly dictate the terms of any agreement. This brings us back to the conundrum faced by many smaller states wishing to become more engaged in the global economy.

Nation-states devoid of the ability to act unilaterally in such areas for the benefit of their own citizens face clear choices. They can choose the status quo, which only serves the needs of their people so long as they do not clash with the 'national interests' of more powerful players. They can, however, choose to seek relationships that respect their legal and moral status among the broader community of nations. Such a relationship requires a greater appreciation of each other's relative situation or status, as well as a conscious commitment to not allowing power inequities to unduly skew practical progress.

More simply put, each nation-state's status within the broader framework must rest solely on the legitimacy of their incorporation – that they are, indeed, a legally recognized national entity. By definition, this means that attributes of economic and political power, or territorial possessions should not be a calculation within this metric. It is the promotion of this simple principle that makes the formal participation of the United States within a CFTA problematic.

If one were to extrapolate from the history of American foreign policy a likely scenario for CFTA participation, it is not fantastical to suggest the following. An American administration, mindful of its domestic constituency, as well as the schools of thought that inform her foreign relations, would argue for a special status within the CFTA based on her attributes. While it would be illogical to presume that one member would be granted such leeway, the argument would likely be made that the status also be enjoyed by the more developed nations of a CFTA – Britain, Canada, Australia and New Zealand – a status analogous to the position of the permanent members of the United Nations Security Council. Also, one should assume that such an agglomeration would have powers that would not be extended to other members. In addition, the US position under these circumstances would involve two core principles – the right to unilaterally opt out of agreed positions, and the institutionalization, or entrenchment of this advantageous status.

*African Growth and Opportunities (AGOA) Act*

An example of this approach can be seen with the African Growth and Opportunities Act, passed by Congress in 2000, and designed as a means of promoting trade opportunities for some of the poorest nations in Africa. It specifically targeted "those with a per capita GNP under $1500 in 1998"[164]

---

[164] Mattoo, Dr. Aaditya, Roy, Dr. Devesh, and Subramanian, Dr. Arvind, "*The African Growth and Opportunities Act: The Impact of its Rules of Origin,*" in Commonwealth Trade Hot Topics, Issue No. 22, p.2

allowing them to "...enjoy duty-free access for apparel made from fabric originating anywhere in the world until 30 September 2004."[165]

The stated motives behind AGOA were laudable, and certainly not out of keeping with the goals that a future CFTA would have:

> "The Act authorizes the US President to designate countries as eligible to receive the benefits of AGOA if they are determined to have established, or are making continual progress toward establishing among others market-based economies; the rule of law and political pluralism; elimination of barriers to U.S. trade and investment; protection of intellectual property; efforts to combat corruption; policies to reduce poverty; increasing availability of health care and educational opportunities; protection of human rights and worker rights; and elimination of certain child labor practices."[166]

The effect of this provision was considered to be significant. According to research done by Drs. Aaditya Mattoo, Devesh Roy, and Arvind Subramanian "even on conservative estimates about Africa's supply response, Africa's non-oil exports could be increased by about 8-11 percent. Most of this increase will be accounted for by the apparel sector, which is expected to grow by approximately 8.3%."[167]

While this can no doubt be considered as a step in the right direction, the US initiative, as in previous cases, falls short of greater success as it tries to appease the special interests that hold sway in Congress. Indeed, initiatives

---

[165] Ibid., p.2
[166] Ibid., p.1
[167] Ibid., p.6

171

like AGOA are as much about catering to particular economic players in the United States as they are about encouraging growth and development in poorer regions. In analyzing the impact of AGOA on those African states who qualify for its treatment, Mattoo, Roy, and Subramanian found that:

*"The medium-term gains could have been much greater if AGOA had not imposed certain conditions and not excluded certain items from its coverage. The most important condition is the stringent rule-of-origin, i.e., the requirement that exporters source certain inputs from within Africa or the United States. The estimates suggest that the absence of these conditions would have magnified the impact nearly five-fold, resulting in an overall increase in non-oil exports of US$0.54 billion compared with the US$100 - US$140 million increase that is expected in the presence of these restrictions."*[168]

Indeed, they go on to say that "...AGOA as it is now will yield only 19-26 percent of the benefits that could have been provided if access had been unconditional. Nearly eighty percent of this shortfall is accounted for by the rules of origin requirements in the apparel sector, which will significantly reduce exports below sub-Saharan Africa's full potential."[169]

For its CFTA partners, there is the uncertainty as to whether the access granted to American markets is assured. For members from the developing world, there is simply the perpetuation of the elements of the status quo that those societies find problematic today – domination from one or more great

---

[168] Ibid., p.6
[169] Ibid., p.7

powers extending beyond economic concerns into areas of public policy and civil society.

This scenario, of course, presumes that the United States would be interested in joining a CFTA, by whatever means it is constituted. Given that there is significant vocal opposition to America signing any new agreements – and some who advocate abandoning existing ones – one cannot discount the real possibility that the political will in America does not exist in sufficient measure to place it on the national agenda.

In fact, beyond the WTO, the preference for American decision makers in matters of trade is to pursue bilateral agreements. In terms of preserving and consolidating American economic power, it is an intelligent strategy. It has the effect of defining world trade in terms of a 'hub and spoke' model, with the US serving as the centre point. As good as it may be for America, it is still a highly unstable model, as its strength and vitality hinges on the one player who acts as the 'hub.' Weakness in the US economy sends reverberations throughout the model. It is, in essence, a recreation of the economic model of Imperial Britain, and as we saw in that case, a trauma to the central power can be amplified in its impact throughout a trading regime, and not in a positive fashion.

Despite the caveats to US participation in a CFTA, there are significant benefits to closer cooperation on trade, commerce and investment. The United States is not a malevolent power, but merely a highly self-interested one. An acceptance of this reality, as well as the need to preserve the principles of a CFTA's composition, merely compels us to be specific about the relationship we seek with America.

It is the opinion of the author that US membership within a CFTA would be potentially disruptive and would throw the organization's broader agenda into disarray. In order to provide the necessary flexibility within a relationship – allowing both the United States and the CFTA members to preserve the integrity of their national prerogatives – it is recommended that the relationship be articulated in the context of a US-CFTA trade agreement.

Such an approach provides real advantages for both parties. For the United States, there is the prospect of enhanced trade opportunities in a potential market of 2 billion people that share a common language, legal tradition, and a commitment to democracy and human rights. For CFTA members, there are the opportunities that come from access to the single largest national economy and capital market in the world.

In pursuing a cooperative relationship at this level, CFTA members assume, collectively, a position of relative equality. Toward this end, it becomes less likely that member states would be required to assume the majority of compromises and concessions. Conversely, an American administration negotiating with a unified CFTA, would be more insulated from the political pressure that emanates from the Congress, or the special interests who use the threat of withholding political support for legislators in order to push for concessions that go beyond what one would objectively consider guarantees for free and fair trade.

Dr. Henry Kissinger puts it best when he writes that "there has been too great a tendency to identify cooperation with concurrence with an American agenda, too much American domestic legislation being applied to close allies in their own countries; too little understanding of the needs of societies adjusting to the loss of their previous preeminence. A more sensitive

American policy is essential."[170] This, however, is for the American people, through their representatives, to decide. Whether or not the United States takes a different tack in its dealings, it will not be due to any measure or directive that the Commonwealth - either individually, or in concert – takes.

With or without the United States, Commonwealth nations can determine their own place in the world, and how to orient their own relationships. A CFTA can be the expression of a commonly defined mutual interest in development and prosperity. Should a CFTA come to fruition, it is almost assured that American cooperation and a potential partnership would come into being. It would be hoped that when such events come to pass, what we are left with is a far more productive, and respectful, relationship.

---

[170] Kissinger, Dr. Henry, "*Does America Need A Foreign Policy? Toward a Diplomacy for the 21st Century,*" (New York: Simon & Schuster, 2001), p.82

Chapter 13

# CFTA AND THE WTO

The great majority of nations of the world are signatories to, and members of, the World Trade Organization. In doing so, they have agreed to two fundamental rules: first, to commit themselves to the greater effort of trade liberalization; and, second, not to engage in trading practices that are expressly forbidden by the WTO. Indeed, this allowance was first codified under GATT Article XXIV, which was "designed to ensure that free trade arrangements lend, on balance, to growth in world trade and can thus be considered building blocks of a more open world trading system."[171]

---

[171] Preeg, Ernest H. "*The Compatibility of Regional Economic Blocs and the GATT,*" Annals, AAPSS, 526, March 1993, p.165.

The existence of NAFTA, the EU, CARICOM, ECOWAS and other trade pacts already affirms that nothing in the rules of the WTO negates or precludes the formation of a CFTA.

Critics may point to the experience of "Empire Preferential" trade in the early 20th Century and conclude that such an agreement would not be allowed to stand by the WTO today. This opinion would be correct. So how a CFTA treaty would be considered any differently?

The difference has less to do with how CFTA members behave toward each other than how the CFTA, as a whole, would relate to economies outside its membership. "Empire Preferential" did not so much lower tariffs within the British Empire as it did collectively raise tariffs against non-Empire states. The WTO forbids this practice, and allows nations to seek redress through their trade tribunals.

To be consistent with WTO rules and obligations, a CFTA would be free to lower or eliminate duties and tariffs internally. What it cannot do is impose higher duties and tariffs on non-CFTA states, or perform what could be considered as bloc protectionism.

This is not to say that the CFTA, as an organizational structure, or individual member states forgo the right to redress, whether it be related to health and safety standards, or in response to dumping or discriminatory tariffs or duties by non-CFTA states.

Those levers remain. Indeed, they become much more effective when used in concert with other CFTA states. While nothing in the CFTA should compel member states to coordinate their trade policy with non-members through a Secretariat, it would be a resource available if two or more CFTA states saw it as beneficial.

Indeed, it can be argued that a lack of adequate resources, such as policy research and diplomatic support mechanisms, are the single biggest challenge to developing nations participating in the WTO. Amrita Narlikar points out that of the 24 countries who do not have a permanent presence at the WTO, 15 are members of the Commonwealth.[172] This is all the more disconcerting as the WTO arrives at its policies through a process of consensus decision-making, which "as opposed to unanimity, means simply that no member present at the meeting formally objects to the decision...These countries cannot object to the so-called consensus that various bodies of the WTO arrive at in their everyday workings."[173] Even those developed nations that actively participate in the trade body's deliberations do so with certain disadvantages. The average size of a WTO delegation from a developed country is 7.38 versus 3.51 for developing countries.[174] As a result, many nations with a permanent delegation find themselves spread too thin, especially when there are overlapping meetings, and they are forced to choose which one is most vital to their national interests – even if a compelling case could be made for either one.

It is evident that the lack of resources places a great disadvantage on those nations that can least afford it. Indeed, one can argue that it is mainly through adequate resources and strong diplomatic representation that developing nations can overcome natural disadvantages and broker satisfactory outcomes.

---

[172] Narlikar, Amrita, "*The Politics of Participation*," The Round Table #364 (2002), p. 174
[173] Ibid., p. 174
[174] Ibid., p. 174

Also, we must remember that a CFTA should not require any adherence by its members to a code of exclusivity. No member should be prevented from negotiating bilateral, or indeed, multilateral, agreements outside the realm of the CFTA. Independent nations must reserve the right to conduct their foreign and trade policy according to the precepts characteristic of any independent and sovereign state – the only exception being where outside parties wish to conclude "CFTA-wide agreements," where the assent of the entire membership would be needed.

In this respect, one can view a CFTA not as a hindrance, but as an aid to the WTO in its larger work. Commentators such as John O'Sullivan argue that, under certain circumstances, the Commonwealth "may be uniquely placed to forge a new consensus on trade."[175] Reasons for this, he argues, include:

- The Commonwealth has, among its ranks some of the largest exporters of capital, such as Britain, and some of the most capital-hungry economies such as Malaysia, India, Hong Kong and Singapore;

- Commonwealth members are to be found in all the major trading blocs: Britain is in the EU, Canada in the North American Free Trade Area, and Australia in the Cairns Group. Any new trade consensus forged in the Commonwealth would have advocates in all the big trade battalions.

---

[175] O'Sullivan, John, "*World trade's next frontier: The Commonwealth may be uniquely placed to forge a consensus,*" National Post. Don Mills, Ont.: Jun 9, 2000. pg. A.18

Because of this, O'Sullivan adds that "It is therefore more aware than a rich man's club such as the European Union of the common interests linking different economies and so more keen to seek compromises reflecting those interests."[176]

This, of course, is the central challenge of Commonwealth nations within the context of WTO negotiations – creating a consensus from such an economically disparate group that, in turn, must find favour within an even more diverse body.

Some may actually argue that those interests may not be easily reconciled within the WTO framework to begin with. In particular, as many developing nations push for movement on issues of development, some see the organization courting the risk "of two traditional causes of institutional failure--over-expansion and over-reach."[177]

The argument follows that "as pressure to address the social dimension of globalization builds (driven by concerns over inequality of income and access to basic public services such as clean water), there is a tendency to look for effective international institutions--thus, Doctors without Borders worked very hard and succeeded in putting public health issues on the WTO agenda. The consequence, it was suggested, is that the WTO is becoming the

---

[176] Ibid., pg. A.18
[177] Curtis, John M., and Ciuriak, Dan, "*Towards Half Time in the Doha Development Agenda*", in Trade Policy Research 2003, (Ottawa: Minister of Public Works and Government Services Canada), 2003, p.13

"World Everything-but-Trade Organization" or perhaps the "World Bargaining Organization"."[178]

It is because many issues that are either not related to trade liberalization, or have a peripheral impact, are front-loaded onto the negotiations that consensus is such an ephemeral goal. That is to say, in many respects, the WTO runs into the dilemma reflected in the adage that 'if one tries to be all things to all people, they end up becoming nothing to anyone.'

The problem, again, may not be so much a reluctance to address development issues as it is either a lack of appreciation of their importance, or a systemic inadequacy to address them effectively. As John M. Curtis and Dan Ciuriak point out:

> "*Development is not very well understood, with views about appropriate approaches differing considerably. Practitioners have found it necessary to approach development issues on a case-by-case basis, tailoring programs to individual circumstances and adjusting the conditions tied to assistance from one agreement to the next as things are found to work or not to work...this is not exactly an approach suitable for an organization trying to set multilateral rules.*"[179]

They add "there is after all no consensus on how to interpret development objectives in terms of trade negotiations. For one thing, trade

---

[178] Curtis, John M., and Ciuriak, Dan, "*Towards Half Time in the Doha Development Agenda*", in Trade Policy Research 2003, (Ottawa: Minister of Public Works and Government Services Canada), 2003, p.13
[179] Ibid., p.10

deals involve a reciprocal exchange of benefits; but development does not--who is on the other side of the deal?"[180]

Again, we must return to what role the Commonwealth can play in advancing trade that is both free and fair. As Sir Nicholas Bayne points out:

> *"Part of the response to globalization concerns what Commonwealth countries do nationally. Part of it concerns what Commonwealth members do among themselves. But a third, very important part concerns what the Commonwealth – if it so chooses – can do collectively to influence the broader international system, so that it spreads the benefits of globalization among all countries and not just among rich ones."*[181]

Bayne suggests that the Commonwealth begin a tradition of meetings of the organization's trade ministers, much in the way that national finance ministers consult one another, in order to advance shared concerns through shared resources and coordinated positions.[182]

As an intermediary step, it is a useful suggestion that, if pursued, would address many of the problems previously outlined. Moreover, it could, if successful, provide a 'clarion call' for other nations, industrialized and developing alike, who feel equally concerned about these issues, but may be reluctant to act at the risk of isolation.

---

[180] Ibid., p.10
[181] Bayne, Sir Nicholas, *"Durban 1999: The Commonwealth Response to Globalization,"* The Round Table #353 (2000), p.32
[182] Bayne, Sir Nicholas, *"Durban 1999: The Commonwealth Response to Globalization,"* The Round Table #353 (2000), p.34

Developing a nurturing a 'Commonwealth bloc' within the WTO would, under those circumstances, provide some of the benefits of a CFTA, but there would be a limit to how much benefit would accrue.

Regardless of how much coordination takes place within the ranks of the WTO, it is still a body that is broader than the Commonwealth, and one cannot be guaranteed that the 'Commonwealth agenda' would succeed, or that any Commonwealth bloc would hold together. This last point is altogether important as such an agglomeration would need to resist pressure from two major economic powers, the United States and the European Union, but also from other significant players, such as China, Japan, and Russia. Maintaining unity in the face of pressure from one, or more, of these powers may be difficult, especially when individual Commonwealth states have important bilateral relationships with such nations – such as Canada and the United States, Britain and the rest of the EU, or Singapore and China. Under certain circumstances, major trading powers not supportive of the 'Commonwealth agenda' may see the advantage in exploiting cleavages in the bloc – and not necessarily on matters related to international trade.

Also, in investing all of its focus and resources in the WTO, the Commonwealth adopts, by default, an 'all or nothing' strategy. Success at Geneva would be welcomed and celebrated, but a defeat on key trade issues would leave Commonwealth members empty-handed, and no better off than if they had never made the attempt.

Indeed, they may find themselves worse off, considering the damage that may have been done by such an open and public 'dividing and conquering.' Under those conditions, it might be difficult to solicit the support for a revisitation of a particular issue, or the building of a coalition for some other initiative.

For the long term health and stability of the global trading system, it is important to be engaged in the WTO and its processes. Commonwealth nations must not step back from this important forum. We should not, however, overestimate its ability to deliver an overarching agreement or consensus that is acceptable to both the industrialized and developing world alike. Breakthroughs are bound to be particularly difficult to reach and slow in coming. They may offer little substantive value as well.

In this respect, we can see the existence of a CFTA not only as a strong, unified lobby for its members' interests, but also as a catalyst for the cause of trade liberalization, able to take action where no broader international consensus exists.

*Chapter 14*

## CFTA AND THE EU

Potential challenges and opportunities for co-operation between a CFTA and the EU rest primarily on one issue – the status of the United Kingdom.

While it has not been eluded to previously, it is fully understood that Britain's current status within the EU makes its participation highly improbable. It can, however, be argued that the present state of that relationship has not yet made the enterprise impossible.

It is understood that the British public are conflicted over their role in the European project. Not only is there much debate over whether or not Britain should embrace a greater integration, there is much discussion on specific policies. Some debate the value of the Common Agricultural Policy (CAP) to Britain's farmers. Some question whether or not Scotland's fishing industry can be rescued by withdrawing from the Common Fisheries Policy

(CFP). On the biggest issue, whether or not to replace sterling with the Euro, public opinion is almost evenly divided.

The debate does not appear to be whether or not Britain has a future with Europe. It does, however, appear to centre on what the nature of that relationship will be. Regardless of where individual Britons stand on the EU, both perspectives present their own unique opportunities and potential risks. In reality, neither side can guarantee that their best case scenario will come to pass.

Under its treaty obligations, Britain is precluded from seeking and negotiating such trading relationships. External trade at this level falls under the jurisdiction of the EU. Also, since joining the EEC in the early 1970's, the British economy has integrated with Europe to such an extent that severing this link could do serious damage to the UK economy. That being said, the loss of Britain from the EU would be equally detrimental to the rest of the Union. It would be deprived of one of its largest contributors and a significant source of capital and investment.

Britain's reluctance to immediately adopt the Euro as its official currency belies the conflicted view of many in the UK. While seeing the benefits of free access to EU markets, many are skeptical of the political and bureaucratic structures that seem to go in hand.

It could, therefore, be argued that a suitable compromise would be for Britain to be free to redefine its relationship with Europe. A new UK/EU Free Trade Treaty would sever the political and institutional integration, yet preserve access to markets and capital for both parties.

Britain would, in a practical sense, continue to enjoy the benefits of EU trade, yet reserve the right to conclude other agreements and arrangements, such as a CFTA. It would, however, be required to remove itself from the formal political structures of the EU, as well as the monitoring and regulatory powers the EU exercises internally.

Indeed, it is recognized that such an agreement would be based on the interest of both parties – Britain and the EU – to pursue such ends. Only an affirmation of this new status by each of the aforementioned parties would encourage the UK to seriously consider participating in a CFTA.

Given current political realities, it would be exceedingly difficult for Britain to show leadership in the initial formation of a CFTA. Redefining her role in Europe would be a precondition. This, of course, seems unfortunate when one looks at a parallel case of a EU member who has not only been able to retain substantive ties to its former colonies, but has allowed those ties, and the obligations that go with them, to the whole of the Union – that of the "Franc Zone."


*The "Franc Zone"*

Even as European nations such as France have been particularly determined about Britain making a choice between her former colonies and the EU, that choice has not been universally forced. Indeed, France presents a clear example of a EU member that has retained significant economic ties to her former colonies, through the support of the "Franc Zone."

There are 14 African countries, 12 of which were former French colonies, who belong to the 'Franc Zone', and thus, share a common currency, the CFA Franc. The CFA Franc was created on December 26, 1945, the day when France ratified the Bretton Woods agreement and made its first convertibility declaration to the IMF.

At that time, CFA stood for "Franc des Colonies Françaises d'Afrique" (Franc of the French Colonies of Africa). In 1958, it became the Franc de la Communauté Française d'Afrique (Franc of the French Community of Africa).

The Zone is, in reality, two zones operating under separate central banks. Benin, Burkina Faso, Côte d'Ivoire, Guinea Bissau, Mali, Niger, Senegal and Togo which form the West African Economic and Monetary Union (WAEMU), share a common central bank, the Central Bank of West African States (BCEAO). Cameroon, Central African Republic, Congo, Gabon, Equatorial Guinea and Chad form the Central Africa Economic and Monetary Community (CEMAC), whose common central bank is the Bank of Central African States (BEAC).

Both zones call their currency the CFA Franc, but for WAEMU, it stands for *"franc de la Communauté Financière d'Afrique"* (Franc of the African Financial Community), while for BEAC states, it represents *"franc de la Coopération Financière en Afrique Centrale"* (Franc of Financial Cooperation in Central Africa).

Despite the apparent differences in administration, both versions of the CFA Franc have equal value, and are subject to the same rules. They are still guaranteed by the French Treasury, and, up until the introduction of the Euro, pegged to the value of the French franc. After 1999, the value of the

CFA Franc is set against the Euro. This is accomplished through an operational account, opened by the French Treasury in the name of the African Central Banks of the franc zone, on which the latter must deposit at least 65% of their external reserves.

When the Maastricht treaty was ratified, French officials had argued that the monetary agreements of the franc zone could not be affected. The position was that because the guarantees for the CFA francs were made through the French Treasury, and not the *Banque de France*, there was no abrogation. This was based mostly on their interpretation of Article 109, Paragraph 5 of the treaty. This allowed member states the freedom to conclude international agreements as long as they are not contrary to the EU's authority over economic and monetary union. It was argued that the treaty did not prevent members from granting loans to whomever they like, and that the potential volume of debit from the operational accounts would be too small to have a major effect on the EU's external reserves.

This view was not necessarily shared by other EU states who felt that the agreement fell under the purview of the first paragraph of Article 109. This asserted that it is the prerogative of the Council of Ministers of the Union to conclude formal agreements concerning any exchange rate mechanisms for the euro against non-EU currencies. A compromise was found on the basis of paragraph 3, according to which the EU could enter into such agreements subject to a qualified majority vote of the Council of Ministers, on recommendation of the Commission, and after consultations with the European Central Bank (ECB). On November 23, 1998, the EU's Council of Ministers confirmed that France could maintain the agreements that bound it to the franc zone.

The agreement, however, included a significant change. Any major change in the membership of the franc zone, or the question of CFA Franc convertibility, would be subject to a decision of the Council of Ministers, on the recommendation of the EU Commission, and after receiving the opinion of the ECB. France has the duty of informing its EU partners about the functioning of the zone. If the member states of the Franc Zone were to decide to devalue one or the other of the two CFA francs, which is their right, France would have to inform *a priori* its European partners.

This system worked reasonably well until the latter half of the 1990's. As a precondition of membership in the European Monetary Union, the French government tied the value of the franc to the German Mark. This led to an appreciation in the CFA francs against the US dollar and several European currencies. Unfortunately, this occurred at the same time as the market prices of many of their principal exports dropped, In addition, there was increased competition in industrial production from within Africa, as other nations had initiated currency devaluations – sometimes rather aggressively. Before long, the franc zone was posting negative growth.

What helped turn the corner were three events: the devaluation of the two CFA francs by half in the beginning of 1994 – an inevitability because of the almost full suspension of external financing; an unexpected growth in the prices of export commodities; and the resumption of external borrowing privileges.

It is important to note that the countries of the Franc Zone figure among those ACP states that were signatories to the Lomé and Cotonou Conventions. While one may only speculate on the connection, it is worth noting that Franc Zone members fared better economically than other Lomé countries not part of the regime.

The Franc Zone represents a case where not only did a EU member state maintain significant economic ties to its former colonies, it was able to extend and develop it into a pan-European responsibility. European critics of British participation in a CFTA would be on shaky ground being opposed to a policy that they have already allowed France an exemption to pursue.

## *A CFTA without Britain?*

It might seem rather strange to see the development of a Commonwealth trade zone without the leadership of Britain. Today's Commonwealth, however, is an association of sovereign states that have had the freedom to exercise their own foreign and economic policies recognized for the last seven decades. British participation is helpful, but it is certainly not a precondition.

To wait for Britain's leadership in creating a CFTA is to wait for the British people to, once and for all, resolve the conflict in their minds over their status in Europe. Without this, the authority of Britain to move into an agreement is in doubt, and the support of the people is unclear at best. The unity of voice and vision that is prerequisite would not exist. In the meantime, other Commonwealth partners interested in exploring this idea waste precious time and opportunity in not pushing forward of their own volition.

Having said that, if the British people expressed their preference for an economic relationship with Europe that did not include political harmonization; and if prominent Commonwealth states such as Australia,

Canada, and New Zealand were prepared to enter into a preliminary agreement; and if other prominent Commonwealth actors such as South Africa and Singapore were sufficiently public in their interest; then UK participation would ensure not only the success of the initial effort, but would give a CFTA the critical mass to grow and develop further.

The problem with the current debate is that it casts the choice as part of some 'zero sum' outcome – Europe or the Commonwealth. It is regretful that many do not see the two relationships as potentially complimentary, and that rather than argue discarding one for the other, energy and focus would be put toward reconciling them.

*Chapter 15*

"NETWORK TRADING"

While the nations of the CFTA would, in themselves, constitute a free trade zone, it is important to emphasize its impact on the broader global community. Member states of the CFTA would function as partners in a larger enterprise, but this does not negate their acting independently. Indeed, the greater success of a CFTA would be predicated on member states assuming such initiative.

Because it is not intended for a CFTA to be an exclusive arrangement, member states would be free to pursue other relationships, as well as nurture existing agreements.

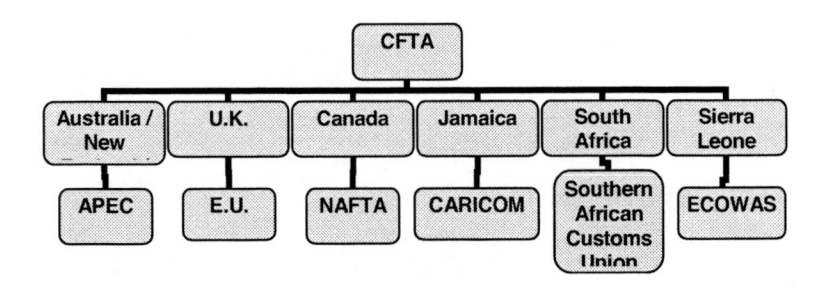

```
                        ┌──────┐
                        │ CFTA │
                        └──────┘
   ┌────────┬──────┬────────┬─────────┬──────────┬─────────┐
┌────────┐ ┌────┐ ┌──────┐ ┌────────┐ ┌────────┐ ┌────────┐
│Australia│ │U.K.│ │Canada│ │Jamaica │ │ South  │ │ Sierra │
│  /New   │ │    │ │      │ │        │ │ Africa │ │ Leone  │
└────────┘ └────┘ └──────┘ └────────┘ └────────┘ └────────┘
    │        │       │         │          │          │
┌────────┐ ┌────┐ ┌──────┐ ┌────────┐ ┌─────────┐ ┌────────┐
│  APEC  │ │E.U.│ │NAFTA │ │CARICOM │ │Southern │ │ ECOWAS │
│        │ │    │ │      │ │        │ │ African │ │        │
│        │ │    │ │      │ │        │ │Customs  │ │        │
│        │ │    │ │      │ │        │ │ Union   │ │        │
└────────┘ └────┘ └──────┘ └────────┘ └─────────┘ └────────┘
```

Figure 3: Schema for a CFTA "Trading Network".

As the diagram shows, many of the existing regional trading blocs have potential CFTA partners within their ranks. Under these conditions, the CFTA would act as the hub of the wheel, creating an informal link between these actors, allowing all parts of the "wheel" to benefit.

Using the above diagram as an example, US companies, through NAFTA, receive national treatment for their Canadian subsidiaries, which would be free to trade within a CFTA. Such would also be the case for EU based companies through their British subsidiaries, and so on.

For the parent companies of these concerns, the increased trade exposure means greater opportunity, which also means increased opportunity for investment. For the CFTA partners that serve as a 'conduit', there is the promise of greater Foreign Direct Investment (FDI), enhancement of infrastructure and the creation of employment and tax revenue.

For CFTA-based concerns the same rules would apply, with the exception that they may find it necessary to establish subsidiaries in particular CFTA states for the expressed purpose of gaining entry into other trading blocs. South African companies, for example, would have to establish a physical presence in Canada to benefit from NAFTA access to the United States.

The benefit from this structure is its stability. Rather than being dependent upon the prospects of one central power, the CFTA will depend equally upon all members. With over 1.7 billion people spread over 53 nations, it is logical to presume that any weakness in the economy of one member state could be offset by gains in another. Also, because of the low levels of industrialization and per capita GDP in many cases, growth rates should remain relatively robust. When one accounts for the other non-CFTA relationships that connect to this network, this system may rely on a significant percentage of the world's trade.

When one considers the scope of a fully implemented CFTA and the 'network' it helps create, it is not out of line to suggest that it could be the means by which the greater WTO agenda is realized.

The real payoff, then, may go beyond how a CFTA transforms its member economies. It may rest on its utility in forcing movement on issues bogged down by great power politics. It seems likely that a US – EU standoff over agriculture in the WTO would not stand if the collective authorities of 1/3 of the world's population decided to take the initiative. Such is the power potential of a CFTA – not to force agreements where there is no consensus or intent, but simply to place its strength behind initiatives that are vulnerable to the actions of few players.

## Chapter 16

## THE WAY FORWARD ?

The process under which a CFTA would take shape, as we have seen, would take an enormous amount of effort, both in the physical structuring, and in the political negotiations to make it possible. It would be a matter of involved negotiations on many economic issues, with more than one party. It would, moreover, be complicated by the need to pursue a dual track – both on political and economic topics.

Throughout this book, we have examined the kind of multilateralism that will be needed to ensure that Commonwealth free trade becomes a practical reality. We have also looked at several initiatives, real and proposed, that have attempted to create the ideal conditions for trade and development. None of these is, admittedly, perfect, and the degrees of success they have enjoyed represent a rather mixed bag. They do, however, constitute a body of information and experiences that champions of this vision would do well to heed.

While one could promote the merits of creating an entirely new organization and structure, it has always been the view of the author that political realities and expediency make preferable the reformation, or expansion, of an existing architecture. It may be the pragmatic recognition of the paradox that when seeking unity, what divides us is just as important as what brings us together. A clean slate does afford a chance to be creative and innovative, but it also throws open the possibility of revisiting past battles and opening old wounds. As a Canadian, I am familiar with the experience of my nation in matters relating to her Constitution, and that it was a far easier task for the founders of my country to have ratified the original draft than it has been for subsequent leaders to amend it in the slightest way. It is my sense that this is not a uniquely Canadian conundrum.

To this end, what is being suggested is not so much a creation of a CFTA from nothing, as the re-engineering of an existing framework along such lines as to eventually evolve into a CFTA. In considering the best way forward, one must acknowledge what a CFTA is meant to achieve, and how it is best served to evolve. Those points have been addressed in the preceding chapters.

We know that a CFTA will, in most likelihood, begin with the four most economically developed Commonwealth states: Australia, Canada, New Zealand, and the United Kingdom (contingent upon how that nation defines its relationship within the EU). We also know that the eventual goal is to create a forum where one can strive to eliminate tariffs, duties, and quotas - excepting areas deemed to be of vital national interest – where each member preserves the basic powers and rights afforded to any sovereign state.

In our exploration of the various types of trade architecture, real and proposed, which relate to the Commonwealth, it appears that one existing trade agreement possesses the necessary attributes – the architecture and the scalability. It also encompasses the trading relationship of two of the four potential founding members of a CFTA.

The Australia-New Zealand Closer Economic Relations Trade Agreement (ANZCERTA) provides proponents of Commonwealth Free Trade the best possible foundation for a larger project that could potentially touch the lives of one-third of humanity. It is a ready, successful, and functioning model that has achieved within its mandate what a CFTA would seek to achieve on a broader scale.

As we have discussed in previous chapters, for a CFTA to effectively be a vehicle for trade liberalization and wealth generation, it will need to incorporate both a Charter of Conduct, as well as a governance mechanism that allows for multilateral participation. ANZCERTA is a viable vehicle for this enterprise, given that it could incorporate many of the suggestions made thus far to make the transition to a pan-Commonwealth organization.

While this presents the easiest option for developing a CFTA, it is far from certain whether it would be a practicality. The viability of such a strategy hinges on two points: first, whether the governments of Australia and New Zealand are supportive of extending membership in the CER beyond the trans-Tasman region; and second, whether they would find a new, more diverse, governance structure conducive to their interests, or if it reflects the original spirit of the founding document.

These are not small issues. The relative size and stature of prospective members is by no means proximate. Admitting Canada into the agreement means bring aboard a nation whose population, and GDP, are almost the equivalent of Australia and New Zealand combined. Again, when one looks to the UK, it almost approximates the combination of the aforementioned three. The obvious concern will be how the disproportionate size of applicant states changes the locus of power, and with it, the relationship that has been created between the founding members.

Notwithstanding these concerns, such a development can be made a practical reality. What is required is a commitment to the principles of equity and of mutual respect as the parties attempt to define their relationship. Australia and New Zealand need to be confident that in inviting others into the CER, that they are not unduly subordinating their own interests, or losing controls that they deem vital to their broader policy interests, both foreign and domestic. Conversely, nations such as Canada and the United Kingdom will be reluctant to agree to any regime that does not afford them a true voice in how the agreement is structured, and what direction it may take in the future.

These concerns and interests are not incompatible. It is not too simplistic to state that the best means of reconciling these concerns is to create parity and equivalency among its signatories. The ANZCERTA, already, is respectful of this idea if one considers that two nations – one being a quarter of the population of its partner – has functioned effectively for over 20 years, and that the Free Trade Area that preceded it since the 1960's had built enough good will between the two to make this last step a reality.

Ideally, then, what might be possible would be the expansion of ANZCERTA to include Canada and Britain, and in doing so, set to work developing the kinds of governance and bureaucratic mechanisms discussed already in previous chapters.

It is not the intention of the author to suggest that this approach will be easy. Rather, that this particular strategy would arguably be easier to implement than other alternatives. Also, there is no intention to presume, or infer, what judgments or policy decisions the principals involved – both within and without the ANZCERTA – may decide to be in their inevitable interest.

Another approach that is equally meritorious of consideration is that put forth by Michael Ancram, Foreign Affairs critic for the British Conservative Party. In a 2003 speech to the Royal Institute of International Affairs, Ancram suggested the creation of "an internal Powerhouse for the Commonwealth," or 'C8.'Comprised of eight states – which would include Australia, Canada, India, South Africa, and the UK – it would be a powerful core that could "more effectively deliver Commonwealth objectives."[183]

Although not specifically oriented toward full trade liberalization, the idea is designed to give greater impetus to cooperation in areas such as education, health care and research, taxation, and agriculture, but to name a few activities. The inception of such a core Commonwealth grouping, in Ancram's view, "would be a political force to reckon with," possessing an "economic strength [that] would give it focused influence on the world economic stage."[184]

This idea, while a step in the right direction, and complimentary to the objectives of a CFTA, is still unclear on how the full slate of C8 nations would be completed, or what their new status of *primus inter pares* will mean

---

[183] Ancram, Rt. Hon. Michael, Q.C., M.P., *"After Zimbabwe, has the Commonwealth still got a purpose?"* Speech at the Royal Institute of International Affairs, Chatham House, London, UK, February 5, 2003

[184] Ibid., February 5, 2003

to the rest of the Commonwealth. Moreover, by anchoring a C8 grouping within the existing Secretariat's architecture, one might speculate on what rule changes would be required to facilitate its activities and enhanced mandate.

These offerings are merely those of a Commonwealth citizen and interested observer who recognizes an opportunity in developing the ideas and work of past leaders and intellectuals. In this modern age of participatory democracy and instantaneous technology, however, the views of interested parties and observers can be made to count. Ideas do matter, and should those ideas have merit, and enjoy a popular support, our modern world affords us the opportunity to promote their development and acceptance.

It would be of great benefit if one or more Commonwealth governments were to adopt the spirit of this idea, if not the actual details of it, as a policy to be pursued with some energy and vigour. That would be, if history is any indication, hopelessly optimistic and somewhat naïve. Such an idea, which admittedly requires no less than a 'paradigm shift' in the way we conduct our economic affairs, will not likely find fertile ground among those who are heavily invested in conventionalism.

So what is the way forward? Simply put, it is to build an association of like-minded people who find merit in the concept, are willing to promote it, and, of course, be constructively critical of it where need be. The best approach is to create a network of national organizations that bring together citizens from all walks of life – political activists of every stripe, industry and professional groups, labour leaders, academia, and the arts to name a few. Drawing from such a diverse cross-section of society ensures two important outcomes – one, the kind of broadly based popular support needed to place

Commonwealth Free Trade on the political agenda in each respective country; and two, to build the kind of expertise, or 'talent pool' necessary to develop the minutiae of how the scheme would work.

Building a network of national groups that undertake research, fundraising, recruitment and promotion, as well as working cooperatively with their counterparts in other Commonwealth jurisdictions, is the best means by which this idea can be brought to the forefront of political discourse in those societies.

These groups, because of their national nature, have a better understanding and appreciation of the political realities within their own jurisdictions. They are best equipped to place the idea in the best possible position for popular support, mindful of the inner workings of local political groups, business and labour organizations, and the media. Also, they can translate the idea into a frame of reference that speaks to the lives of everyday people in a way that a larger effort cannot.

More importantly, from a philosophical standpoint, it is only right and proper that any organized effort to initiate a Commonwealth Free Trade Association be a bottom-up exercise. In the end, such a far-reaching program must have the input of those who will live with its effects. If it is able to yield the degree of economic transformation necessary to be considered a success, then it is imperative that all participants in an economy, from all socioeconomic backgrounds, are given the opportunity to champion, or critique, the idea from the beginning.

Broad-based participation means that the final product of the process will be more properly reflective of society, and the needs and interests of as inclusive a cross-section of the populace as possible.

*Chapter 17*

## CONCLUSION

While the 21st century has barely just begun, we may be able to discern the geopolitical trends that will shape international relations for decades to come. The world's economy is, and will increasingly be, dominated by larger nations, or trading blocs. This does not necessarily mean that minor to medium actors will not see some benefits in some areas, but the occurrence of this is far from assured. As history is a witness, sovereign states can only rely on their own capabilities, the only exception being where common cause can be found among allies.

As Sir Shridath Ramphal, former Secretary-General of the Commonwealth, observed in an address to the Royal Commonwealth Society in London in 2002:

*"Among the many ways future historians may describe the first years of the 21st century is the paradox they presented of a world community desperately in need of acting together, acting multilaterally in the interest of the enduring advance of human society – and one threatened with the emergence of new imperialism and the ascendancy of division, dominion and discord; a world set on a path of human regression. Will it be a history of how humankind chose the path of sustainable progress, or will that history chronicle the beginning of a dark era of human decline towards self-destruction?"*[185]

While it may be tempting for many to characterize this idea as a reaction to the current geopolitical realities – and to some extent, it is – to view Commonwealth free trade as simply some knee-jerk reaction to today's power politics is to miss much of the point. Commonwealth free trade should not be seen so much as what we wish to do to others as it would be what we aspire to do for ourselves. It is about choices, and having the freedom to make them with no other provisos save serving the needs of one's citizens, and being a responsible, cooperative actor in the world. Those seeking to address petty piques and long standing grudges may see, in this concept, the perfect vehicle for settling affairs. To do so, however, erodes the efficacy of the concept and transforms a statement of vision into a platform for the disgruntled and angered. For Commonwealth free trade to become a viable reality, it must be more than this.

The idea of a Commonwealth Free Trade Association, while being a challenging project, should not be seen as an impossible or impractical exercise. As we have seen, the collapse of the British Empire was not a collapse of economics. Indeed, two world wars and a global depression left

---

[185] Ramphal, Sir Shridath, "*Global Governance or a New Imperium: Which is it to be?,*" The Round Table #369 (2003), p.213

the Commonwealth bloc financially anemic, but not defeated. It is only when one factors in other issues – increased competition, inefficiency in colonial administration, lack of a coherent and unified policy, as well as pressure from the United States in post-war settlements – do we see the end of 'imperial preference.'

More important, however, than all these points was the difficulty of redefining the relationship between Britain and the dominions. The larger geopolitical events of the first half of the 20$^{th}$ century literally reversed the relative position of the major players in the Commonwealth. Britain's decline was juxtaposed to the ascendancy of Australia, Canada, New Zealand, and South Africa among others. Economically, the dominions had developed to be major markets, as well as sources of capital in their own right. Through two world conflicts, they had fielded fighting forces that stood on a par with the mother country. Moreover, over a period of decades, these nations had developed unique identities and distinct histories. They inspired their own cultures and their own particular sense of being. This self-awareness was difficult to reconcile with the traditional definition of 'colony.'

The transition from Empire to Commonwealth was more than an official redesignation of the relationship. It was a psychological shift that set the tone for future dealings, even to this day.

The Commonwealth, however, continues to this day to be an important multilateral forum for issues of development, education, social, cultural and technical cooperation. It endures, however, without the structural flaws of its former incarnation. It is an association of free and sovereign peoples, able to exercise their right to self-determination and self-actualization. Freedom to govern one's self means freedom to determine the course of one's community and one's own life. Not only was this transformation necessary to preserve the relationship between Commonwealth states, it is the very thing that enables us today to discuss the possibility of forming a free trade area of its members.

The CFTA, in this sense, should be seen as the guarantor of social prosperity and national independence. The commitment of each nation must be to respect the rights and dignity of its own citizenry and to allow the flow of goods and capital to proceed without bias or prejudice.

A Commonwealth Free Trade Association, if effectively implemented, would serve a pivotal role in the expansion of trade in goods and services globally. Uniquely among all existing or proposed models it offers the vision of a truly global structure – not dominating, but accessing. To those who accept this challenge, there is the promise of greater prosperity and development without sacrificing any of the basic tenets of participatory democracy.

To the world outside the Commonwealth, a CFTA would advance the greater cause of liberalization and the spread of wealth. More prosperity for the peoples of the world allows for more economic opportunity as well as greater stability in domestic and regional politics.

Rather than being considered as a rival trading organization seeking to monopolize world trade and restructure the existing economic order, a CFTA should be seen for what it is – a forum for linking rich and poor nations, and existing trade blocs into a network whose rules and conduct foster good governance, human rights, and the continuing work of the WTO to which all subscribe. Its presence on all continents would position it like no other institution for this purpose.

Success, however, depends on the peoples of the Commonwealth to attain a clear perspective on our shared past, as well as our hope for the future.

Do we continue to believe the fiction that the old economic empire ended not from a confluence of factors – internal and external – but solely from its own incompetence and inefficiency? Do we avoid Commonwealth free trade because of political conditions that have not existed in our lifetimes? Do we, in essence, let our preoccupation with the past handicap our ability to work effectively in the present and in the future?

The very fact that 53 nations have chosen, of their own volition, to be members of the Commonwealth of Nations speaks to the value and utility of the organization. The number of activities and their varied nature demonstrates that Commonwealth members have a demonstrated faith and commitment to preserving existing ties and building new ones.

Our shared history has much to teach us. What makes this moment in time important in advancing this concept is that we are finally at a point where the lessons that history teaches us can finally be appreciated. Both those who once ruled, and those who were ruled, understand that the 'Imperial' relationship only finds life in the books of the past, and the fading memories of a passing generation, soon to disappear altogether.

The world has changed, but so too has our sense of ourselves. Many of us within the Commonwealth may share a British heritage, and be proud of what it represents, but one would be hard pressed to find anyone outside the UK proper who would call themselves a 'Briton' instead of Australian, Canadian, South African, New Zealander, or Indian.

It may be because of the fact that the peoples of the Commonwealth have developed such strong and proud identities amongst themselves, that we can exude the self-confidence necessary to take such a step. In personal terms, it is because I am so proudly Canadian, and secure in that fact, that I can envision myself in a larger Commonwealth project, and not feel threatened or haunted by the past.

A Commonwealth Free Trade Association, founded upon the principles and core values promoted in this work, is not a threat to the sovereignty and independence of any state or any people. If there is such a threat that exists, it would most certainly be at present, where there are few rules for conduct in the international arena, and where might most often makes right. Vulnerability is the greatest threat to any nation or people, whether it be in terms of questions of war and peace, or in terms of economic determination and the ability to set a democratically-derived standard for conduct in the body of a nation.

A CFTA, in many respects, represents a form of 'collective security' for small states and medium powers who risk marginalization in a world where superpowers and supra-national jurisdictions set the international economic and trade agenda to address their own interests.

The days of empire have long ended, and there is much to regret from that legacy. More importantly, however, we are left with the seeds of a new and brighter future. If the peoples of the Commonwealth may be able to build a secure tomorrow for their children, based on the inalienable principles of freedom, democracy, equality and respect, we may partially vindicate our shared history.

If given the proper thought, from its design, through the various phases of implementation, to an eventual completion, a Commonwealth Free Trade Association could bring all peoples closer to a "common wealth."

In summation, the sentiments and ideas being expressed in this work are best represented by the view put forward by Derek Ingram when he stated that:

> *"A changing world means there will always be a need to review what is being done and to cut out an activity from time to time that is no longer relevant or being carried out by others. But the possibility must not be dismissed that the Commonwealth can find itself in a position to launch a major international initiative if the need is evident. Good imaginative ideas will produce the resources when the time comes. The Commonwealth must be ready to think big if the opportunity arises."*[186]

In the end, the concept of Commonwealth Free Trade is a challenge for the Commonwealth, leaders and citizens alike, to do just that. Think big.

---

[186] Ingram, Derek, "*A Much-Too-Timid Commonwealth,*" The Round Table #351(1999), p.505

LIST OF APPENDICES

APPENDIX A: Population (Vital Statistics)*

APPENDIX B: Environment*

APPENDIX C: Economic Statistics*

APPENDIX D: Technology and Infrastructure*

APPENDIX E: Trade and Finance*

APPENDIX F: Private Sector Investment*

APPENDIX G: Information and Information Technology*

APPENDIX H: Global Economic Integration*

APPENDIX I: Governance and Accountability

APPENDIX J: The Fancourt Commonwealth Declaration on Globalisation and People-Centred Development

* all figures taken from World Bank, World Development Indicators, 2004 database –
www.worldbank.org/data/countrydata/countrydata.html

## APPENDIX A: Population (Vital Statistics)

| | Australia | Canada | India | New Zealand | South Africa | United Kingdom |
|---|---|---|---|---|---|---|
| Population, total (millions) | 19.7 | 31.6 | 1000 | 3.9 | 45.3 | 59.3 |
| Population growth (annual %) | 1.3 | 0.9 | 1.6 | 1.5 | -0.1 | 0.1 |
| Life expectancy (years) | 79.2 | n/a | 63.4 | 78.4 | n/a | n/a |
| Fertility rate (births per woman) | 1.8 | n/a | 2.9 | 1.9 | n/a | n/a |
| Infant mortality rate (per 1000 live births) | 6.0 | n/a | 65.0 | 6.0 | n/a | n/a |
| Under 5 mortality rate (per 1000 children) | 6.0 | n/a | 90.0 | 6.0 | n/a | n/a |
| Births attended by skilled health staff - (% of total) | n/a | n/a | n/a | n/a | n/a | n/a |
| Child malnutrition, weight for age (% of under 5) | n/a | n/a | n/a | n/a | n/a | n/a |
| Child immunization, measles (% of under 12 mos.) | 94.0 | n/a | 67.0 | 85.0 | n/a | n/a |
| Prevalence of HIV (Female %, ages 15-24) | n/a | n/a | n/a | n/a | n/a | n/a |
| Net primary enrollment (% of relevant age group) | n/a | n/a | n/a | n/a | n/a | n/a |
| Net secondary enrollment (% relevant age group) | n/a | n/a | n/a | n/a | n/a | n/a |

## APPENDIX B: Environment

| | Australia | Canada | India | New Zealand | South Africa | United Kingdom |
|---|---|---|---|---|---|---|
| Surface area (sq. km.) | 7.7 m | 9.971 m | 3.3 m | 270,000 | 1.2 m | 242,900 |
| Forests (1000 sq. km.) | n/a | n/a | n/a | n/a | n/a | n/a |
| Deforestation (average annual %: 1990-2000) | n/a | n/a | n/a | n/a | n/a | n/a |
| Freshwater resources per capita (cubic meters) | 25021.6 | n/a | 1819.2 | 83016.0 | 1102.7 | 2481.9 |
| CO2 emissions (metric tons per capita) | n/a | n/a | n/a | n/a | n/a | n/a |
| Access to improved water source (% of total population) | n/a | n/a | n/a | n/a | n/a | n/a |
| Access to improved sanitation (% of urban population) | n/a | n/a | n/a | n/a | n/a | n/a |
| Energy use per capita (kg of oil equivalent) | n/a | n/a | n/a | n/a | n/a | n/a |
| Electricity use per capita (kWh) | n/a | n/a | n/a | n/a | n/a | n/a |

## APPENDIX C: Economic Statistics

|  | Australia | Canada | India | New Zealand | South Africa | United Kingdom |
|---|---|---|---|---|---|---|
| GNI, Atlas method (current US$ billion) | 384.1 | 756.8 | 567.6 | 52.2 | 126.0 | 1700 |
| GNI per capita, Atlas method (current US$) | 19530 | 23930 | 530 | 13260 | 2780 | 28350 |
| GDP (current US$ billion) | 409.4 | 834.4 | 510.2 | 58.6 | 159.9 | 1800 |
| GDP growth (%) | 2.7 | 1.8 | 8.0 | 4.3 | 1.9 | 2.2 |
| GDP implicit price deflator (annual % growth) | 2.8 | 2.4 | 3.2 | -1.1 | 5.9 | 3.1 |
| Value added – Agriculture (% of GDP) | n/a | n/a | 22.7 | n/a | 3.8 | n/a |
| Value added – Industry (% of GDP) | n/a | n/a | 25.7 | n/a | 31.0 | n/a |
| Value added – Services (% of GDP) | n/a | n/a | 51.6 | n/a | 65.2 | n/a |
| Exports of goods and services (% of GDP) | 19.6 | n/a | 14.9 | 33.2 | 27.6 | n/a |
| Imports of goods and services (% of GDP) | 22.2 | n/a | 16.9 | 31.6 | 23.7 | n/a |
| Gross capital formation (% of GDP) | 24.1 | n/a | 23.9 | 20.3 | 14.9 | n/a |
| Current revenue, excluding grants (% of GDP) | n/a | n/a | n/a | n/a | n/a | n/a |
| Overall budget balance, including grants (% of GDP) | n/a | n/a | n/a | n/a | n/a | n/a |

## APPENDIX D: Technology and Infrastructure

|  | Australia | Canada | India | New Zealand | South Africa | U.K. |
|---|---|---|---|---|---|---|
| Fixed lines and mobile telephones (per 1000 people) | 1178.4 | 1012.6 | n/a | 1069.8 | 410.5 | 1431.3 |
| Telephone average cost of local call (US$ per three minutes) | 0.1 | n/a | n/a | n/a | 0.1 | 0.2 |
| Personal computers (per 1000 people) | 565.1 | 487.0 | n/a | 413.8 | 72.6 | 405.7 |
| Internet users | 9.5 m | 16.1 m | n/a | 1.9 m | 3.1 m | 25 m |
| Paved roads (% of total) | n/a | n/a | n/a | n/a | n/a | n/a |
| Aircraft departures | 356,300 | 263,900 | N/a | 265,300 | 122,000 | 905,600 |

## APPENDIX E: Trade and Finance

|  | Australia | Canada | India | New Zealand | South Africa | United Kingdom |
|---|---|---|---|---|---|---|
| Trade in goods - share of GDP (%) | 33.5 | 67.1 | 20.8 | 49.0 | 56.6 | 39.9 |
| High technology exports (% of manufactured exports) | 16.5 | 14.3 | 4.8 | 10.1 | 5.1 | 31.4 |
| Foreign direct investment, net inflows in reporting country (current US$) | 16.6 b | 20.5 b | 3.0 b | 823.1 m | 6.1 b | 29.2 b |

## APPENDIX F: Private Sector Investment*

|  | Australia | Canada | India | New Zealand | South Africa | United Kingdom |
|---|---|---|---|---|---|---|
| Domestic credit to private sector (% of GDP) | 89.8 | 82.2 | 32.6 | 118.1 | 131.7 | 142.6 |
| Foreign direct investment (% of GDP) | 4.1 | 2.9 | 0.6 | 1.4 | 0.7 | 1.8 |
| Investment in infrastructure projects w/private participation: Telecommunications (US$ millions) | n/a | n/a | 14950.0 | n/a | 10654.8 | n/a |
| Investment in infrastructure projects w/private participation: Energy (US$ millions) | n/a | n/a | 9680.5 | n/a | 1244.3 | n/a |
| Investment in infrastructure projects w/private participation: Transport (US$ millions) | n/a | n/a | 1969.1 | n/a | 1874.1 | n/a |
| Investment in infrastructure projects w/private participation: Water and Sanitation (US$ millions) | n/a | n/a | 216.0 | n/a | 212.5 | n/a |

## APPENDIX G: Information and Information Technology

|  | Australia | Canada | India | New Zealand | South Africa | United Kingdom |
|---|---|---|---|---|---|---|
| Daily newspapers per 1,000 people | 293 | 159 | 60 | 362 | 32 | 329 |
| Radios - per 1,000 people | 1,999 | 1,047 | 120 | 997 | 338 | 1,446 |
| Televisions per 1,000 people | 731 | 700 | 83 | 557 | 152 | 950 |
| Cable subscribers per 1,000 people | 72.2 | 267.9 | 38.9 | 7.1 | 0.0 | 64.1 |
| Personal computers per 1,000 people | 515.8 | 459.9 | 5.8 | 392.6 | 68.5 | 366.2 |
| Personal computers in education | 706,794 | 1,019,436 | 238,667 | 195,483 | 364,722 | 1,824,106 |
| Internet users – thousands | 7,200 | 13,500 | 7,000 | 1,092 | 3,068 | 24,000 |
| Information technology expenditures - % of GDP | 10.7 | 8.7 | 3.9 | 14.4 | 9.2 | 9.7 |
| Information technology expenditures (per capita US$) | 1,939 | 1,960 | 19 | 1,835 | 269 | 2,319 |

## APPENDIX H: Global Economic Integration - 2002

|  | Australia | Canada | India | NZ | S. Africa | UK |
|---|---|---|---|---|---|---|
| Trade in goods (% of GDP) | 33.5 | 67.1 | n/a | 49.0 | 56.6 | 39.9 |
| Ratio of commercial service exports to merchandise exports (%) | 25.8 | 14.4 | 49.9 | 35.1 | 14.8 | 44.0 |
| Gross private capital flows (% of GDP) | 20.0 | 13.4 | n/a | 9.2 | 10.1 | 60.3 |
| Gross foreign direct investment (% of GDP) | 6.3 | 7.3 | n/a | 4.0 | 1.4 | 23.8 |

## APPENDIX I: Governance and Accountability*
### (percentage rank 1 – 100)

|  | Australia | Canada | India | New Zealand | South Africa | United Kingdom |
|---|---|---|---|---|---|---|
| Voice and accountability | 94.4 | 94.9 | 60.6 | 97.0 | 70.7 | 93.9 |
| Political stability | 89.7 | 87.0 | 22.2 | 95.1 | 42.7 | 73.5 |
| Government effectiveness | 92.8 | 94.8 | 54.1 | 95.9 | 69.1 | 97.9 |
| Regulatory qu: | 94.8 | 93.8 | 43.8 | 96.4 | 69.1 | 97.9 |
| Rule of law | 95.4 | 93.8 | 57.2 | 96.4 | 59.8 | 94.3 |
| Control of corruption | 93.8 | 95.9 | 49.5 | 99.0 | 67.5 | 94.3 |

Source: D. Kaufmann, A. Kraay, and M. Mastruzzi 2003: "*Governance Matters III: Governance Indicators for 1996 – 2002*" in World Bank, World Development Indicators 2004.

Note: The governance indicators presented here reflect the statistical compilation of responses on the quality of governance given by a large number of enterprise, citizen and expert survey respondents in industrial and developing countries, as reported by a number of survey institutes, think tanks, non-governmental organizations, and international organizations.

## APPENDIX J:

## The Fancourt Commonwealth Declaration on Globalisation and People-Centred Development

In today's world, no country is untouched by the forces of globalization. Our destinies are linked together as never before. The challenge is to seize the opportunities opened up by globalization while minimizing its risks.

On the positive side, globalization is creating unprecedented opportunities for wealth creation and for the betterment of the human condition. Reduced barriers to trade and enhanced capital flows are fuelling economic growth.

The revolution in communications technologies is shrinking the distance between nations, providing new opportunities for the transfer of knowledge and the development of skills-based industries. And technological advance globally offers great potential for the eradication of poverty.

But the benefits of globalization are not shared equitably. Prosperity remains the preserve of the few. Despite the progress of the past fifty years, half the world's population lives on less than two US dollars per day. Many millions live in conditions of extreme deprivation. The poor are being marginalized. Expanded capital flows have also brought with them the risk of greater financial instability, undermining the hope that a commitment to open markets can lift the developing world, especially the least developed countries, out of poverty and debt.

The persistence of poverty and human deprivation diminishes us all. It also makes global peace and security fragile, limits the growth of markets, and forces millions to migrate in search of a better life. It constitutes a deep and fundamental structural flaw in the world economy.

The greatest challenge therefore facing us today is how to channel the forces of globalization for the elimination of poverty and the empowerment of human beings to lead fulfilling lives.

The solution does not lie in abandoning a commitment to market principles or in wishing away the powerful forces of technological change. Globalisation is a reality and can only increase in its impact. But if the benefits of globalization are to be shared more widely, there must be greater equity for countries in global markets.

We call on all nations fully to implement the Uruguay Round commitments to dismantle barriers to trade for the mutual benefit of all. Moreover, recognizing in particular the significant contribution that enhanced export opportunities can make for reducing poverty, we call for improved market access for the exports of all countries, particularly developing countries, and the removal of all barriers to the exports of the least developed countries.

Strong export growth remains a key element in the ability of developing countries to improve their living standards to the levels enjoyed in the industrialized world. We support efforts that would enable developing countries to build up their skills and manufacturing capacities, including the production and export of value-added goods, so as to enhance growth and achieve prosperity.

Likewise, we urge that the forthcoming Ministerial Meeting of WTO to launch the next round of global negotiations on trade be one with a pronounced developmental dimension, with the aim of achieving better market access in agriculture, industrial products and services in a way that provides benefits to all members, particularly developing countries. The Round should be balanced in process, content and outcome.

We fully believe in the importance of upholding labour standards and protecting the environment. But these must be addressed in an appropriate way that does not, by linking them to trade liberalization, end up effectively impeding free trade and causing injustice to developing countries.

We also call on the global community to establish innovative mechanisms to promote capital flows to a wider number of countries; and to urgently initiate reform of international financial architecture to minimize financial instability and its impact on the poor.

We believe that the elimination of poverty is achievable – but only if we take determined and concerted actions at national and international levels. We reiterate our commitment to work for a reversal of the decline in official development assistance flows. Urgent action is also required to tackle the unsustainable debt burden of developing countries, particularly the poorest, building on the recent initiatives agreed internationally. We believe such development assistance must be focused on human development, poverty reduction and on the development of capacities for participating in expanding world markets for goods and capital. Above all, we recognize the responsibilities of national governments to promote pro-poor policies and human development.

If the poor and the vulnerable are to be at the centre of development, the process must be participatory, in which they have a voice. We believe that the spread of democratic freedoms and good governance, and access to education, training and health care are key to the expansion of human capabilities, and to the banishment of ignorance and prejudice. Recognising that good governance and economic progress are directly linked, we affirm our commitment to the pursuit of greater transparency, accountability, the rule of law and the elimination of corruption in all spheres of public life and in the private sector.

We are concerned at the vast gap between rich and poor in the ability to access the new technologies, at the concentration of the world's research resources in market-driven products and processes, the increasing tendency to claim proprietary rights on traditional knowledge, and at bio-piracy. We call on the world community to use the opportunities offered by globalization for adopting practical measures for overcoming these challenges; for example, by extending the benefits of global medicine research through the provision of drugs at affordable prices to the poor in developing countries.

We welcome the spread of ideas, information and knowledge in building civil support for social equality, and in opposing all forms of discrimination and other injustices based on ethnicity, gender, race and religion. But, while better communications have increased human contact, there is for some a growing sense of social exclusion and a general failure of moral purpose. Persistence of inequalities faced by women, continued high levels of youth unemployment, lack of adequate support systems for the aged, children and the disabled in many parts of the world and increased threats to the diversity of cultures and beliefs all contribute to the undermining of just and stable society. We therefore call for a renewed commitment to eliminate all forms of discrimination and to take measures that promote respect for the diverse languages, cultures and beliefs, and traditions of the world, which enrich all our lives.

Recognizing that the full exploitation of the opportunities for development created by globalization is not possible without security, political stability and peace, we commit ourselves, in partnership with civil society, to promote processes that help to prevent or resolve conflicts in a peaceful manner, support measures that help to stabilize post-conflict situations, and combat terrorism of all kinds.

Good governance requires inclusive and participatory processes at both national and international levels. We call on the global community to search for inclusive processes of multilateralism which give a more effective voice in the operations of international institutions to developing countries, and which recognize the particular vulnerabilities of small states.

We believe that the Commonwealth, an association of diverse sovereign nations reflecting different stages of development and united by common values, has a vital role to play in promoting consensus at national and international levels and in providing practical assistance for the creation of capacities needed to promote people-centred development. At the threshold of a new millennium, we look to the

Commonwealth, and its family of organizations, to contribute significantly to making the above aspirations a reality.

Fancourt
George, South Africa
14 November 1999

# BIBLIOGRAPHY

Abdullah, Saiful Azhar, "*Rough Waters ahead for the Commonwealth,*" Business Times, Kuala Lumpur, 2003 December 10.

Ancram, Rt. Hon. Michael, Q.C., M.P., "*After Zimbabwe, has the Commonwealth still got a purpose?*" Speech at the Royal Institute of International Affairs, Chatham House, London, UK, 2003

Bayne, Sir Nicholas, "*Durban 1999: The Commonwealth Response to Globalization,*" The Round Table #353 (2000).

Beatty, Hon. Perrin, "*Beyond NAFTA: The rules for global engagement,*" Plant Magazine, Vol. 63, Issue 1, 2004 January 19.

Beauchesne, Eric, Wire Feed – Business, Statistics, CanWest News Service, Don Mills, Ontario, Canada, 2004 April 28

Blair, Rt. Hon. Tony, "*Prime Minister's statement to the Commonwealth Business Forum – Wednesday 22 October 1997,*" http://www.number-10.gov.uk/output/Page1065.asp, 2003 September 19.

Brown, Rt. Hon. Gordon, "New Global Structures for the New Global Age," The Round Table #349 (1999)

Commonwealth Business Council – Enhancing Trade, http://www.cbcglobelink.org/cbcglobelink/CBCPage.jsp?headingId=1 (2004 March 18)

Commonwealth of Australia, Department of Foreign Affairs and Trade, "*Closer Economic Relations – A Background Guide to the Australia-New Zealand Economic Relationship*", February 1997.

Curtis, John M., and Ciuriak, Dan, "*Towards Half Time in the Doha Development Agenda*", in Trade Policy Research 2003 , (Ottawa: Minister of Public Works and Government Services Canada), 2003

Davenport, Michael, "*ACP-EU negotiations*," in Commonwealth Trade Hot Topics, Issue No. 16

Economist.com/Global Agenda, "*What's the Commonwealth For?*", London: Dec 8, 2003.

Ferguson, Niall, "*Empire:: The Rise and Demise of the British World Order and the Lessons for Global Power,*" (New York: Basic Books), 2002.

Forbes.com, "*Global 2000 ranking database*," www.forbes.com, 2004 August 5.

French, David, "*Rethinking the Commonwealth Institute*," The Round Table #352 (1999).

Hargittai, Eszter and Centeno, Miguel Angel, "*Defining a Global Geography*," American Behavioral Scientist, Vol. 44, No. 10, June 2001.

Hinds, Allister, *"Britain's Sterling Colonial Policy and Decolonization, 1939 – 1958,"* (London: Greenwood Press), 2001.

Ingram, Derek, "*A Much-Too-Timid Commonwealth*," The Round Table #351 (1999)

Kaul, Mohan, "*The Commonwealth and Globalization*," The Round Table #364 (2002)

Kennedy, Paul, *"Rise and Fall of the Great Powers: Economic Change and Military Conflict from 1500 to 2000,"* (London: Fontana Press), 1988.

Kissinger, Dr. Henry, *"Does America Need A Foreign Policy? Toward a Diplomacy for the 21st Century,"* (New York: Simon & Schuster), 2001.

Kunkel, John, "*Australian trade policy in an age of globalisation,*" Australian Journal of International Affairs, Vol. 56, No. 2, 2002.

LaFeber, Walter, *"The American Age,"* (New York: W.W. Norton and Company), 1994

Lavin, Deborah, *"From Empire to International Commonwealth,"* (Oxford: Clarendon Press), 1995.

Lloyd, Lorna, "*Loosening the Apron Strings: The Dominions and Britain in the Interwar Years,*" The Round Table # 369 (2003)

Martin, Rt. Hon. Paul "*Canada and the Commonwealth Business Forum,*" The Round Table #349 (1999)

Mattoo, Dr. Aaditya, Roy, Dr. Devesh, and Subramanian, Dr. Arvind, "*The African Growth and Opportunities Act: The Impact of its Rules of Origin*," in Commonwealth Trade Hot Topics, Issue No. 22

Mbuende, Dr. Kaire M., "*ACP-EU Future Trade Relations: Challenges and Opportunities for Eastern and Southern African Countries*," in Commonwealth Trade Hot Topics, Issue No. 15

McKenzie, Francine, "*Redefining the Bonds of Commonwealth, 1939 – 1948: The politics of preference*", (Houndmills, Basingstoke, Hampshire: Palgrave Macmillan) 2002.

Narlikar, Amrita, "*The Politics of Participation*," The Round Table #364 (2002).

Nevin, Tom, "*Nepad – what is it and what can it really do?*", African Business, April, 2003.

O' Sullivan, John, "*World trade's next frontier: The Commonwealth may be uniquely placed to forge a consensus*":[National Edition], National Post. Don Mills, Ont.: 2000 June 9.

Otieno-Odek, J., "*Europe and Sub-Saharan Africa Beyond Lomé IV Convention*," University of Nairobi, Kenya, http://www.oneworld.org/ecdpm/lome/otieno.htm , 2003 August 26.

Persaud, Bishnodat, "*Developing Countries and the New Round of Multinational Trade Negotiations*," The Round Table (2000), #353.

Pettigrew, Hon. Pierre, *"Reconciling the Spirit and Ethics of Liberalism in the 21st Century"*, Trade Policy Research 2003, (Ottawa: Minister of Public Works and Government Services Canada), 2003

Preeg, Ernest H.., "*The Compatibility of Regional Economic Blocs and the GATT*," Annals, AAPSS, 526, March 1993.

Ramphal, Sir Shridath, "*Global Governance or a New Imperium: Which is it to be?*," The Round Table #369 (2003).

Rooth, Tim, "*Economic Tensions and Conflict in the Commonwealth, 1945 – c.1951*," Twentieth Century British History, Vol. 13, No. 2, 2002

Rosenberg, Mark and Hiskey, Jonathan T., "*Changing Trading Patterns of the Caribbean Basin*," in Annals, AAPSS, 533, May, 1994.

Rowley, Charles K., Thorbecke, Willem, and Wagner, Richard E., "*Trade Protection in the United States*" (Aldershot: Edward Elgar Publishing Ltd.), 1995

Sacks, Michael Alan, Ventresca, Marc J., and Uzzi, Brian, "*Global Institutions and Networks: Contingent Change in the Structure of World Trade Advantage, 1965 - 1980*," American Behavioral Scientist, Vol. 44, No. 10, June 2001.

Schott, Thomas, "*Global Webs of Knowledge – Education, Science, and Technology*," American Behavioral Scientist, Vol. 44, No. 10, June 2001.

Schreuder, Deryck M., "*A Commonwealth for the 21$^{st}$ Century*," The Round Table #367 (2002).

Trinidad and Tobago Chamber of Industry and Commerce – "*Caricom countries need to keep to their agreements*," February 07, 2002, http://www.chamber.org.tt/article_archive/column/070202.htm

Vaile, Hon. Mark, "*Australia-New Zealand CER Still a Benchmark 20 Years On*," Media Release, 27 March 2003 - MVT24/2003

World Development Indicators database, www.worldbank.org, 2004 July 15

# INDEX

## A

Aden, 36
Afghanistan, 36
Africa, v, 28, 32, 33, 34, 38, 39, 40, 41, 42, 43, 44, 45, 46, 52, 55, 57, 58, 61, 66, 71, 78, 79, 88, 89, 107, 112, 113, 114, 115, 117, 119, 120, 121, 125, 127, 144, 149, 150, 169, 170, 171, 187, 189, 191, 199, 204, 210, 211, 212, 213, 214, 215, 216, 222, 226
African Growth and Opportunities (AGOA) Act, 169
African, Caribbean and Pacific (ACP), 86
Alaska, 36
Alberta, 78
America, 2, 14, 16, 24, 32, 34, 35, 36, 40, 41, 43, 58, 71, 107, 109, 112, 127, 160, 161, 162, 168, 172, 174, 225
American exceptionalism, 159, 161
Ancram, Rt. Hon. Michael, 199, 223
Anglo-Burmese Wars, 37
Anglo-Egyptian Sudan, 40
Anglosphere, 157, 158
Anguilla, 108
Antigua, 34, 79, 107, 108
Arabia, 36, 166
Argentina, 44
ASEAN, 123, 144
Asia, 24, 32, 56, 98
Assembly of Caribbean Community Parliamentarians (ACCP), 109
Athabaska Tar Sands, 78
Atlantic Charter, 56, 57, 62
Australia, v, 16, 28, 32, 37, 40, 41, 43, 44, 52, 54, 57, 58, 61, 75, 76, 78, 79, 83, 97, 98, 102, 104, 121, 122, 123, 124, 125, 126, 144, 150, 169, 178, 190, 196, 197, 198, 199, 204, 210, 211, 212, 213, 214, 215, 216, 224, 228

## B

Bahamas, 79, 108
Bangladesh, 75
Bank of Central African States (BEAC), 187
Barbados, 34, 79, 107, 108, 109, 110
Bayne, Sir Nicholas, 181, 223
Beatty, Hon. Perrin, 167, 223
Belize, 34, 79, 108, 110

Benin, 187
Bennett, James C., 158
Bermuda, 33, 108
Black, Lord, 158
Blair, Rt. Hon. Tony, 20, 223
Boers, 38
Borden, Sir Robert, 95
Borneo, 37
Brazil, 14, 101
Bretton Woods, 187
Brisbane, 3
Britain, 6, 16, 28, 29, 31, 32, 34, 35, 36, 37, 38, 39, 40, 41, 42, 43, 44, 46, 47, 48, 49, 51, 52, 53, 54, 55, 56, 57, 58, 59, 60, 61, 62, 63, 64, 97, 100, 102, 104, 105, 106, 128, 129, 151, 158, 169, 172, 178, 182, 184, 185, 186, 190, 198, 204, 225
British Columbia, 163, 164, 165
British Empire, 8, 10, 28, 31, 32, 33, 35, 36, 40, 41, 45, 46, 47, 48, 51, 56, 57, 64, 73, 176, 203
British Guiana, 107
British North America, 35, 36, 40, 41, 43
British North Borneo Company, 37
British Overseas Territories, 46
British South Africa Company, 38
British Virgin Islands, 108
British West Indies (BWI) Federation, 106
Brooke, James, 37
Brown, Rt. Hon. Gordon, 6, 17, 151, 155, 223
Brunei, 37
Bryce, R.B., 100
Burkina Faso, 187
Burma, 32, 37, 42

**C**

C8, 199
Cairns Group, 79, 125, 126, 127, 128, 129, 178
Cameroon, 39, 46, 187
Canada, iv, 16, 28, 29, 33, 34, 35, 36, 40, 41, 43, 44, 52, 54, 55, 57, 58, 59, 60, 61, 68, 69, 75, 76, 78, 79, 83, 90, 95, 96, 97, 98, 99, 101, 102, 103, 104, 105, 121, 125, 126, 136, 137, 140, 144, 147, 150, 151, 154, 155, 163, 164, 166, 167, 168, 169, 178, 179, 180, 182, 191, 194, 196, 197, 198, 199, 204, 210, 211, 212, 213, 214, 215, 216, 223, 224, 225, 227
Cape Colony, 38, 40
Cape of Good Hope, 38
Cape Town, 38
Caribbean Basin Initiative, 111

231

Caribbean Development Bank (CDB), 108
Caribbean Free Trade Association (CARIFTA), 107
CARICOM, v, 106, 108, 109, 110, 111, 112, 113, 114, 144, 176
Cayman Islands, 108
Central African Republic, 187
Central Bank of West African States (BCEAO), 187
Ceylon, 37, 42
Chad, 187
Chamberlain, Joseph, 8
Chennai, 3
China, 13, 28, 36, 44, 113, 145, 182
Churchill, Sir Winston, 56, 57
Cilliers, Jakkie, 119, 120
Ciuriak, Dan, 147, 179, 180, 224
Colombo Plan, 102
Colonization, 33
Common Agricultural Policy (CAP), 88, 128, 184
Common External Tariff, 110
Common Fisheries Policy (CFP), 185
Commonwealth Business Council (CBC), 20
Commonwealth Free Trade Association (CFTA), ii, iv, 8, 10, 11, 12, 15, 17, 21, 22, 23, 31, 52, 61, 70, 71, 72, 73, 74, 75, 76, 77, 78, 79, 81, 84, 85, 90, 91, 92, 93, 94, 100, 101, 102, 104, 116, 125, 132, 137, 140, 141, 142, 143, 144, 145, 146, 147, 148, 149, 150, 151, 152, 153, 154, 155, 156, 157, 158, 159, 160, 161, 166, 167, 168, 170, 171, 172, 173, 176, 184, 185, 187, 188, 189, 190, 192, 193, 194, 198, 199, 200, 202, 206, 207, 209, 210, 211, 213, 214, 215, 218, 224, 226
Commonwealth Fund for Technical Cooperation (CFTC), 19
Commonwealth Institute, 65, 224
Commonwealth of Learning (COL), 19
Commonwealth of Nations, 7, 8, 11, 15, 18, 41, 45, 73, 206
Commonwealth Science Council (CSC), 19

Commonwealth Secretariat, 19, 21, 87, 89, 91, 132, 133, 138, 153
Concert of Europe, 2
Congo, 187
Cooper, Andrew, 126
Cullen, Dr. Michael, 127
Curtis, John M. 180
Curtis, Lionel, 8

## D

Davenport, Michael, 91, 224
de Gaulle, Charles, 103
Diefenbaker, Rt. Hon. John, 95, 96, 97, 100, 103, 105
Dominica, 108
Dominions, 41, 45, 59, 60, 225
Durham, Lord, 35, 40, 55
Durham Report, 55

## E

East India Company, 33, 36, 37, 38
East Indies, 37
ECOWAS, v, 176
EEC, v, 44, 62, 102, 185
Egypt, 39, 40, 55
Elizabeth II, 43, 45, 79
Empire Preferential, 46, 176
Equatorial Guinea, 187
Europe, 2, 14, 16, 33, 44, 62, 63, 71, 88, 89, 97, 98, 102, 104, 105, 107, 113, 127, 185, 186, 190, 191, 226
European Central Bank (ECB), 188
European Commission, 89
European Union (EU), 124

## F

Falkland Islands, 44
Fancourt Declaration, 66
Ferguson, Niall, 47, 52, 53, 54, 56, 57, 63, 224
Foreign Direct Investment (FDI), 193
Franc Zone, 186, 187, 189, 190
France, 33, 35, 38, 39, 48, 105, 128, 150, 186, 187, 188, 189, 190
Frechette, Myles, 112
French, David, 65
Fukuyama, Francis, 1

## G

Gabon, 187
Gambia, 33
Gandhi, Mahatma, 42
GATT, v, 61, 85, 101, 122, 129, 175, 227
George VI, 45
German East Africa, 40

Germany, 39, 48, 51, 52, 54, 56, 97
Ghana, 43
Gibraltar, 33, 44
Globalization, 16, 23, 28, 50, 66, 181, 223, 225
Gold Coast, 33, 43
Grant, George, 104, 105
Grant, Dr. George 59
Great Depression, 53
Grenada, 79, 108, 110
Gross Domestic Product (GDP), 75
Guyana, 108

**H**

Haiti, 109
Henry II, 41
Hinds, Allistair, 47, 53, 55, 225
Hong Kong, 32, 37, 44, 178
Hughes, Charles Evans, 159

**I**

Iceland, 55
Imperial Conferences, 41
India, 13, 16, 17, 28, 32, 33, 36, 37, 38, 42, 43, 45, 61, 75, 77, 80, 83, 145, 150, 178, 199, 210, 211, 212, 213, 214, 215, 216
Indian War of Independence, 36
Ingram, Derek, 18, 208, 225
International Labour Organization (ILO), 3
International Monetary Fund (IMF), 151, 153
Iran, 32
Iraq, 32, 40, 55
Ireland, 41, 55
Irish Free State, 41, 45
Israel, 32, 40, 73

**J**

Jamaica, 29, 33, 34, 79, 107, 108, 110
Japan, 13, 28, 56, 98, 124, 182
Jinnah, Muhammad Ali, 42
Johannesburg, 79
Johnston, Eric, 101

**K**

Kaul, Mohan, 15, 16, 49, 50, 225
Kenya, 39, 88, 89, 119, 226
Kissinger, Dr. Henry, 173, 174, 225
Kowloon, 37
Kunkel, John, 123, 225

**L**

LaFeber, Walter, 159, 160, 225
Laurier, Sir Wilfrid, 95
League of Nations, 32, 38, 39, 40, 42

Libya, 120
Lloyd, Lorna, 59
Lloyd, Sir Selwyn,
    104
Lomé
    Conventions,
    5, 86, 88, 90,
    93, 143
London, 3, 44, 47,
    48, 52, 53, 57,
    79, 80, 83, 87,
    89, 91, 96, 105,
    132, 158, 199,
    202, 223, 224,
    225
Lower Canada, 35,
    40
Luce, Henry, 160

**M**

Macdonald, Sir
    John A. 95
Thomas L.
    Macdonald, 98
Macmillan, Rt.
    Hon. Harold,
    57, 98, 104,
    226
Mahdi of Sudan,
    39
Malaya, 36, 37, 43
Malaysia, 16, 77,
    79, 145, 178
Malcolmson, Dave,
    120

Mali, 187
Mandela, Nelson,
    44
Marlborough
    House, 18, 132
Martin, Rt. Hon.
    Paul, 151, 154,
    155, 225
Mattoo, Dr.
    Aaditya, 169,
    170, 171, 226
Mbeki, Thabo, 114
Mbuende, Dr.
    Kaire M., 87,
    89, 91, 149,
    226
Menzies, Sir
    Robert, 97, 98
MERCOSUR, 123
Mexico, 29, 85,
    103, 112, 167
Montserrat, 34, 108
Mountbatten, Lord
    Louis, 42
Mozambique, 46,
    73, 75
Mutual Aid
    Agreement, 57
Myanmar, 37

**N**

Namibia, 44
Napoleonic Wars,
    2

Narlikar, Amrita
    133, 177, 226
NASDAQ, 80
Natal, 38, 40
National Africa
    Company, 39
National Policy, 95
Nauru, 38
NEPAD, v, 114,
    115, 116, 117,
    118, 119, 120,
    121
Netherlands, 37, 38
Nevis, 34, 79, 108
New Amsterdam,
    34
New Brunswick,
    36
New England, 33
New Guinea, 38,
    79
New Hampshire,
    34
New Hebrides, 38
New South Wales,
    37
New Zealand, 28,
    32, 37, 40, 41,
    44, 45, 52, 57,
    58, 61, 71, 75,
    76, 79, 83, 98,
    102, 104, 121,
    122, 123, 124,
    125, 127, 144,
    150, 169, 191,
    196, 197, 198,

204, 206, 214, 224
Newfoundland and Labrador, 33, 36, 45, 57
Nicaragua, 111
Niger, 39, 187
Nigeria, 39, 78, 119
Nkrumah, Kwame, 43
North America, v, 16, 24, 32, 34, 35, 36, 40, 41, 43, 71, 104, 113, 178
Nova Scotia, 33, 36

**O**

OECD, v, 86, 117, 126, 132
O'Neill, Tip, 3
Ontario, iv, 35, 36, 40, 167, 223
OPEC, 78
Opium Wars, 37
Orange Free State, 38
Organization of Eastern Caribbean States (OECS), 108
O'Sullivan, John, 158, 178, 179

Ottawa, 3, 53, 94, 97, 98, 104, 137, 140, 147, 179, 180, 224, 227
Ottawa Agreements, 53, 94, 97
Ottoman Empire, 40, 52

**P**

Pakistan, 42, 45, 61, 145
Palestine, 32, 40
Pearl Harbor, 58
Penang, 36
Persaud, Bishnodat, 20, 21, 226
Pettigrew, Hon. Pierre, 136, 137, 140, 227
Pilgrims, 33
Poland, 128
Portugal, 32, 55
Progressive Conservative party, 95
Puerto Rico, 109

**Q**

Quebec, 33, 35, 36, 40, 69, 70, 99
Queensland, 37

**R**

Ramphal, Sir Shridath, 143, 202, 203, 227
Reciprocity Treaty, 95
Rhodes, Cecil, 38
Rhodesia, 38, 43
Rio de Janeiro, 101
Robinson, Arthur N.R., 110
Roosevelt, Franklin D., 57
Roy, Dr. Devesh, 170
Royal Niger Company, 39
Russia, 2, 13, 182

**S**

Sabah, 37
Sacks, Michael Alan, 24, 27, 29, 249
Sandiford, Erskine, 109
Sarawak, 37
Saudi Arabia, 166

Schott, Thomas, 25, 249

Schreuder, Deryck M., 17, 228
Scotland, 70, 184
Senegal, 114, 187
Sierra Leone, 39, 75, 150
Singapore, 16, 32, 77, 144, 178, 182, 191
Softwood Lumber, 164
Somaliland, 39
South Africa, 28, 38, 41, 44, 45, 55, 57, 58, 61, 66, 69, 71, 78, 79, 88, 114, 119, 125, 127, 144, 150, 191, 194, 199, 204, 206, 215, 222
South African War, 38
South Australia, 37
South Carolina, 34
Spain, 32, 33, 44
Sri Lanka, 37, 42
St. Kitts, 79, 108
St. Lucia, 79, 108
St. Vincent, 79, 108
Sterling Area, 30, 53, 55, 61, 94

Subramanian, Dr. Arvind, 169, 170, 171, 226
Sudan, 40, 43, 55
Suez Canal, 40
Sullivan Principles, 71
Sutton, Paul, 90, 113
Sydney, 37, 79, 80

**T**

Tanganyika, 40
Tasmania, 37
Taylor, Ian, 126
Thatcher, Baroness, 157
Togo, 187
Togoland, 39
Toronto, 79, 80, 102
Trans-Jordan, 40
Transvaal, 38
Trinidad and Tobago, 107, 108, 110, 228
Tuvalu, 17, 79

**U**

Uganda, 39, 119
United Kingdom, 17, 41, 45, 56, 75, 76, 79, 95, 96, 100, 105, 121, 144, 184, 196, 198, 210, 213
United Nations, 3, 17, 42, 140, 150, 169
United States, ii, vi, 2, 3, 13, 15, 24, 28, 29, 32, 33, 35, 51, 54, 56, 57, 58, 60, 61, 62, 63, 71, 75, 77, 81, 95, 96, 98, 100, 101, 111, 113, 124, 126, 145, 157, 158, 159, 160, 161, 162, 164, 165, 167, 168, 169, 171, 172, 173, 174, 182, 194, 204, 227
Upper Canada, 35, 40
USSR, vi, 13
Uzzi, Brian, 24, 27, 29, 249

**V**

Vaile, Hon. Mark, 124, 228
Ventresca, Marc J., 24, 27, 29, 249

Virginia, 33, 34

**W**

Wade, Abdoulaye, 114
War of 1812, 35
West African Economic and Monetary Union (WAEMU), 187

West Indies, v, 32, 33, 34, 43, 106
Western Australia, 37, 40
Whitehall, 59, 95
World Bank, 15, 76, 77, 132, 144, 153, 209, 216
World Trade Organization (WTO), 3, 15

World War I, 31, 32, 39, 42, 43, 47, 48, 84
World War II, 42, 43, 84

**Z**

Zanzibar, 39
Zimbabwe, 43, 118, 119, 120, 139, 199, 223
Zoellick, Robert, 164

ISBN 1-41204277-1